Jossey-Bass Teacher

JOSSEY-BASS TEACHER PROVIDES EDUCATORS with practical knowledge and tools to create a positive and lifelong impact on student learning. We offer classroom-tested and research-based teaching resources for a variety of grade levels and subject areas. Whether you are an aspiring, new, or veteran teacher, we want to help you make every teaching day your best.

From ready-to-use classroom activities to the latest teaching framework, our value-packed books provide insightful, practical, and comprehensive materials on the topics that matter most to K–12 teachers. We hope to become your trusted source for the best ideas from the most experienced and respected experts in the field.

Breakthroughs
in Literacy

TEACHER SUCCESS STORIES
AND STRATEGIES, GRADES K-8

Susan E. Israel
and Contributors

JOSSEY-BASS
A Wiley Imprint
www.josseybass.com

Published by Jossey-Bass
A Wiley Imprint
989 Market Street, San Francisco, CA 94103-1741—www.josseybass.com

Readers should be aware that Internet Web sites offered as citations and/or sources for further information may have changed or disappeared between the time this was written and when it is read.

Limit of Liability/Disclaimer of Warranty: While the publisher and author have used their best efforts in preparing this book, they make no representations or warranties with respect to the accuracy or completeness of the contents of this book and specifically disclaim any implied warranties of merchantability or fitness for a particular purpose. No warranty may be created or extended by sales representatives or written sales materials. The advice and strategies contained herein may not be suitable for your situation. You should consult with a professional where appropriate. Neither the publisher nor author shall be liable for any loss of profit or any other commercial damages, including but not limited to special, incidental, consequential, or other damages.

Jossey-Bass books and products are available through most bookstores. To contact Jossey-Bass directly call our Customer Care Department within the U.S. at 800-956-7739, outside the U.S. at 317-572-3986, or fax 317-572-4002.

Jossey-Bass also publishes its books in a variety of electronic formats. Some content that appears in print may not be available in electronic books.

Library of Congress Cataloging-in-Publication Data

Breakthroughs in literacy : teacher success stories and strategies, grades k–8/Susan E. Israel and Contributors.
    p. cm.
  Includes bibliographical references and index.
  ISBN 978-0-470-37182-4 (pbk.)
  1. Language arts (Elementary)—Curricula. 2. Language arts (Middle school)—Curricula.
  3. Literacy—Study and teaching (Elementary)—United States. 4. Literacy—Study and teaching (Secondary)—United States. I. Israel, Susan E.
  LB1576.B599 2009
  372.6' 044—dc22

                                                                        2009015719

Printed in the United States of America

FIRST EDITION

PB Printing 10 9 8 7 6 5 4 3 2 1

Contents

🌿 PART TWO
Motivation: The Right Book Can Make a Difference

🌿 PART THREE
Engagement: Multisensory Experiences

PART FOUR
Transformation: Learning Together

🌿 PART FIVE
Conclusion

Introduction:
Why Teacher Stories?

CLASSROOM TEACHERS, SPECIAL EDUCATION TEACHERS, teacher educators, reading specialists, literacy coaches, and even parents can all gain new ideas and approaches for helping children learn to read and write from reading success stories from today's classrooms. The idea for this book came when Addie, an experienced graduate student in my "Phonics, Spelling and Word Studies" course, was sharing a story with me about one of her fourth-grade students who had been a reluctant reader. I recall Addie entering the classroom right before class started. She was always enthusiastic, but on this particular day she seemed especially eager to tell me something. Paraphrased from my memory at the time of our conversation, Addie explained:

"I was so excited today. For the first time a student shared with me a reading success story. She told me that because I kept on encouraging her to keep reading books and to read books that were especially enjoyable, she finally discovered books that she loves, and all because of me!"

I loved how Addie referred to this as a "reading success story." It was like she was telling me, "Look, something I did made all the difference in the world to a child." Her story stuck with me, primarily because a teacher had shared something with me that was working rather than something that was not.

Breakthroughs in Literacy is a collection of powerful stories authored by a diverse group of people who have devoted much of their lives to working with struggling students. Although most of the authors were teachers in general education classrooms when their stories took place, some were reading specialists or literacy coaches, while others were special education teachers, ESL teachers, or even tutors. Many of them are now university professors.

The authors were invited to contribute stories because of their many years of working with children on literacy learning and finding success along the way. They were asked to submit personal narratives about a meaningful experience where they felt their teaching made a difference in setting an individual student, or group of students, on the path to achievement. Although the authors were given a set of guidelines, they were encouraged to write their stories as if they were sharing them in the teachers' lounge or over the phone with a colleague.

The guidelines for writing these stories included the following criteria:

- *Personal reflections about reading success:* Try to identify what worked for you in the particular learning situation and what you think you could have done differently.
- *Explain how the success was realized:* Describe why and how you made a difference. Reflect on what helped you understand how the transformation started. Identify strategies you employed.
- *Lessons to learn:* In closing each story, summarize the insights and understandings gained so the reader can learn. Each lesson should be placed in context with the learner and the situation.

Retrospective personal narrative is the appropriate writing style for the authors to convey this type of message. Rather than being bound to a scholarly approach, citing relevant theory and research, the storytelling format allows the authors to freely communicate their thoughts, reflections, and insights, as well as the breakthrough strategies that lead to their teaching success.

In the stories, the authors describe their experiences with individual students who had been having difficulty in either reading or writing or who posed a particular instructional challenge. Some are resistant or underperforming readers, some are special education students, and others are English language learners. Many of the students face particular learning barriers, whether fear of not being accepted by peers, deficits in oral language, or diagnosed learning disabilities. Some of the students described suffer problems of poverty and homelessness; others are gifted but have come to dislike reading or writing. As you will see, many of the students in these stories have hidden talents that had never been discovered by anyone.

Goals of the Book

Because it is important for educators to be guided by research-based practices, this book shows readers the outcomes of research-based strategies by having teachers explain why and how they carried out particular instructional approaches. In many cases, the authors found they had to try unusual or unconventional instructional strategies. In each story, you will read about an authentic experience and the author's insights as to the approach that fueled the success with individual students. Whether it is a story about how a child was taught to read or about a particular strategy or program that worked well, the goal is to enable you to use these experiences to reflect on your own approach to teaching literacy. The stories bring multiple viewpoints and perspectives to questions that have always been asked by those in the literacy field:

- What is the best way to teach reading to a struggling learner?
- What is the best way to teach writing to a struggling learner?

Many of the stories spotlight the use of writing, not just as a tool for supporting and inspiring reading but as an essential attribute for converging ideas and expressing understanding of skills and content interpretations.

As a former university professor who continues to work with teachers, I seem to spend a lot of my time trying to help teachers feel good about what they do. I have learned that teachers need to self-discover, through instructional inquiry and reflection, what it is they are doing well. Focusing on what they are doing well helps them realize or affirm why they are teachers. Teachers need affirmation that their work can make a difference. Teacher success stories need to be documented to help other teachers learn and think differently about what they do and can do, to give them hope, courage, and inspiration that they can succeed with their students as well. It is my goal to help you use the stories in this book not only as a tool to discover instructional strategies that you might try but also as a way to help you identify your own reading success stories and share them with others. My personal request would be that you not hide your success stories. We need to hear them. The stories in this volume have been written with humility. They are written from the heart, as you will read, but they are also written with the goal of sharing a success story to help others.

By having multiple teachers describe successes that were memorable to them, my desire is that you will feel as if you are sitting next to each of the authors yourself, listening intently and with a goal of learning new ways of thinking and teaching.

Overview of the Book

The book is divided into four main parts, with stories in each part focusing on the following breakthrough themes:

Part One   Connection: Knowing the Learner
Part Two   Motivation: The Right Book Can Make a
    Difference
Part Three   Engagement: Multisensory Experiences
Part Four   Transformation: Learning Together

Part One focuses on breakthroughs in reading and writing that resulted from application of learner-centered teaching strategies, especially practices emphasizing knowing the learner and involving the student in collaboration. Too often, we think learning has to be done individually. The connections described in these stories demonstrate the power of collaborative learning to motivate students when they are given opportunities to work together. Teachers can work collaboratively with students, and children can support each other to achieve literacy success. The stories invite reflection on the following questions:

- How do I feel when working with others to learn new things?
- What types of collaborative connections can I make to allow students to work together?
- Does my classroom environment allow for moments of social-learning engagement?

Part Two focuses on breakthroughs in motivation that can result when children are provided with meaningful literature selections. In many of the stories, the teachers describe how they enable the children themselves to discover books that are important to them and that invite them to experience the reading world. What is wonderful about these stories is the way the teachers used their own literacy interests and talents to motivate the students. The stories invite reflection on the following questions:

- Do I have specific types of personal reading materials that I can share with my students to make a breakthrough in their thinking and learning?
- Are there talents that I have that can be used as a tool to promote inquiry learning and investigation?
- Is it important for students to have a say in the types of books they read regardless of ability level?

Part Three focuses on breakthroughs that were made possible by having the students engage in hands-on visual, tactile, or other multisensory experiences prior to their reading or writing activities. The stories show that content presented using multisensory methods can enhance achievement and connect with students' individual learning styles. What is interesting about these stories is that the teachers are not afraid to do whatever it takes to motivate the child. They explore interesting and creative ways to teach while at the same time finding success with literacy learning. The stories invite reflection on the following questions:

- What do I want to do to help one child that might speak to teaching in a multisensory method?
- Are there changes I can easily make in my method of teaching today that will promote creativity and reach individual learning styles?
- What will it take to engage my most challenging student?

Part Four focuses on literacy transformations that can occur once the teacher gains a personal understanding of the learner.

The stories in this part feature children who learn in many different ways. The stories demonstrate that unless teachers spend time getting to know their students as individuals and gaining their trust, it can be difficult to engage them in successful learning situations. The stories invite reflection on the following questions:

- How much time do I spend getting to know my students and how best they learn?
- How do I use this information about my students to construct meaningful lessons that appeal to the students' interests while at the same time staying true to meaningful tasks?
- What actions demonstrate a trust-building factor when I am working with struggling students?

Each part of the book includes a separate introduction followed by the stories themselves. At the end of the story section, I share my own thoughts and reflections about the stories as if I were writing in a journal. The stories are further elaborated as follows:

- *Breakthrough Elements*, a section highlighting strategies, practices, and "elements of success" detailed in the stories.
- *Reflection Questions*, a series of study questions encouraging readers to think about their own classroom situation and how their teaching practice might be changed in light of findings in the stories.
- *Lessons Learned*, a summary of themes and discoveries revealing the stories of particular relevance for literacy learning.
- *Breakthrough Actions You Can Take Today*, suggested teaching practices that can be immediately applied in the classroom.
- *Further Reading*, suggested resources to help extend and apply the concepts offered in the stories.

In Part Five, the Conclusion, I draw from the stories to summarize my own views about teaching reading and writing. I suggest seven pathways that teachers can take to ensure that their students engage in successful literacy learning with the goal of achieving a literacy breakthrough.

Susan E. Israel
Fishers, Indiana
June 2009

Acknowledgments

I would like to acknowledge Christie Hakim for an excellent job as editor. I would also like to thank those who were involved with the publication of the book at Jossey-Bass/Wiley: Pamela Berkman, Dimi Berkner, Julia Parmer, Hilary Powers, Chris Wallace, and Carrie Wright. I am grateful for the contributors who did a wonderful job sharing stories of success.

S. E. I.

The Author and Editor

Susan E. Israel, Ph.D., is an independent researcher, writer, and literacy consultant who currently serves as president and CEO of Literacy Media Consulting in Indianapolis, Indiana, where she works with small and large corporations to enhance literacy products. Her special research interests are in the areas of reading comprehension, writing, and child-mind development as it relates to literacy processes. Previously, Israel served as assistant professor at the University of Dayton, and in 2005 she was awarded the university's Outstanding Professor Award. She has also served on the national faculty at the University of Notre Dame Summer Program, where she taught reading and language arts methods. A former elementary teacher, Israel was awarded the 1998 teacher-researcher grant from the International Reading Association (IRA). Having been an active member of the IRA for over a decade, she has served on a number of IRA committees and interest groups and recently was president of the History of Literacy Special Interest Group. In addition, she has been active with the National Reading Conference. Israel has authored, coauthored, or edited more than fifteen books and volumes and is the senior editor of the recently published comprehensive volume *Handbook of Research on Reading Comprehension* (with Gerald Duffy, 2009). Other recent publications include *Teachers Taking Action: A Comprehensive Guide to Teacher Research* (with Cynthia Lassonde, 2008), *Reading First and Beyond* (with Cathy Collins Block, 2005), *Collaborative Literacy* (2006), *Shaping the Reading Field* (2007), *Poetic Possibilities* (2006), and *Quotes to Inspire Great Reading Teachers* (2006).

Susan welcomes your literacy breakthrough stories and comments, and is seeking success stories with special populations and diverse groups, brain injuries, and severe reading disorders. She can be reached at sueisrael@comcast.net or through her Web site, http://home.comcast.net/~sueisrael.

THE AUTHOR AND EDITOR

The Contributors

Terry S. Atkinson, Ph.D., Associate Professor of Reading, East Carolina University, Greenville, North Carolina.

Mary J. Banta, Associate Director for Education, Pastoral Office for Education and Youth Catechesis, Lafayette, Indiana.

William P. Bintz, Ph.D., Associate Professor, College of Education, Kent State University, Kent, Ohio.

Evangelina "Gigi" Brignoni, Ph.D., Assistant Professor, Bilingual Education, ESL, and Literacy, University of Nebraska at Omaha, Omaha, Nebraska.

Vicki S. Collet, Literacy Coach, Poudre School District and Doctoral Student (Reading), New York State University at Buffalo, Buffalo, New York.

Kathy A. Egawa, Ph.D., Literacy Coach, Seattle Public Schools, Seattle, Washington.

Amelia C. Evans, Lead Teacher, Child Development Lab at the McPhaul Center, University of Georgia, Athens, Georgia.

Martha Ford, Teacher and Co-Director, Delaware Writing Project, New Castle, Delaware.

Elizabeth M. Frye, Ed.D., Assistant Professor of Reading, Appalachian State University, Boone, North Carolina.

Sheila K. Gaquin, Deer Harbor, Washington.

Gina A. Goble, Ed.S., New Brunswick Public Schools, New Brunswick, New Jersey.

Lindsay P. Grow, Doctoral Student, Department of Curriculum & Instruction, University of Kentucky, Lexington, Kentucky.

Daniel T. Holm, Ph.D., Associate Professor of Literacy, Indiana University, South Bend, Indiana.

Lisa A. Janes, M.S., Teacher, Central Park Elementary, Mokena, Illinois.

Karen A. Jorgensen, Ph.D., Assistant Professor, Literacy, University of Kansas, Lawrence, Kansas.

Karen J. Kindle, Ed.D., Assistant Professor of Literacy and Reading Education, University of Missouri–Kansas City, Kansas City, Missouri.

Emily Manning, Lee Elementary, Denton, Texas.

Marianne McTavish, Ph.D. Candidate, Language and Literacy Education, University of British Columbia, West Vancouver, British Columbia.

Nina L. Nilsson, Ph.D., Assistant Professor of Education, St. Joseph's University, Philadelphia, Pennsylvania.

Richard M. Oldrieve, Ph.D., Assistant Professor of Early Childhood Education, Bowling Green State University, Bowling Green, Ohio.

Danna Parsons, M.Ed., University of Houston, Houston, Texas.

Limor Pinhasi-Vittorio, Ph.D., Graduate Literacy Coordinator, Lehman College, Bronx, New York.

Monique Poldberg, Teacher, Lake Elsinore Unified School District, Lake Elsinore, California; Teacher-Researcher, Arts and Literacy Integrated in Nebraska and California, University of Nebraska-Lincoln, Lincoln, Nebraska.

Cynthia J. Poston, Ph.D., Reading Intervention Resource/Literacy Coach, Rockwood School District, Saint Louis County, Missouri.

Alexa L. Sandmann, Ed.D., Professor of Literacy, Kent State University, Kent, Ohio.

Mariana Souto-Manning, Assistant Professor, Department of Child and Family Development, and Research Coordinator, Child Development Lab, University of Georgia, Athens, Georgia.

Katie Sullivan, First Grade Teacher, Baker School, Brookline, Massachusetts.

Deborah Vessels, Teacher, St. Louis de Montfort Catholic School, Fishers, Indiana.

Lori Berman Wolf, Ph.D., Associate Professor of Literacy, Adelphi University, Forest Hills, New York.

Pamela L. Wright, Title 1 Specialist, Paducah Public Schools, Paducah, Kentucky.

Angie Zapata, Doctoral Student, University of Texas at Austin, Austin, Texas.

Connection

KNOWING THE LEARNER

About the Stories

Susan E. Israel

OPENING DOORS CREATES OPPORTUNITIES. As teachers and educators, we aim to prepare our students to open and walk through those doors of opportunity. The stories in Part One emphasize why it is important to know students if we are to achieve our targeted instructional goals. As the stories reveal, getting to know students means we must gain an understanding of their learning habits, interests, and motivations. It also means becoming aware of any personal issues that might be blocking their learning, such as lack of confidence, peer frustrations, fears of reading or writing, and possibly behavior or other emotional issues.

In the stories in Part One, teachers share powerful moments in their teaching lives. Although the stories portray students who have difficulty in reading or writing, you will not find a step-by-step method for teaching basic literacy skills. Instead, what you will find are connections of the mind in the form of teaching realizations, or as Karen Kindle in the opening story puts it, the *Aha!* moments.

The stories are written by teachers with varied backgrounds and experiences. Some are first-year classroom teachers; others are reading specialists or special education teachers. Instruction takes place either in or out of the regular classroom.

3

The students are also varied. One you will read about is a struggling reader because she suffers from a traumatic brain injury. Others are described as English language learners, as having varying types of learning disabilities, or as having social or behavioral problems keeping them from literacy tasks. Karen Kindle talks about a child who has repeated first grade and how others have given up on her. Limor Pinhasi-Vittorio discovers how a caring environment can foster learning and trust. Vicki Collet realizes that reading success can be measured in different ways. Cynthia Poston and Angie Zapata share stories about children who are reading below grade level or at the pre-primer stage of learning. Martha Ford closes Part One with a motivational story about giving children space to build trust.

The breakthrough stories you will read in this part have to do with teachers' transforming their thinking about what it means to teach a struggling student how to read and how to write. The task is not just how to read or write; often the child has to acquire the developmental skill necessary to reach the next level of reading and writing. In some cases you will find that the key to progress is the student's ability to master micro-literacy skills like learning "magic *e*" or the teacher's ability to find a story topic that the child finds interesting enough to develop motivation to write. In other cases the key is the discovery of a deeper issue that has nothing to do with reading or writing but keeps the child from allowing the teacher to break through the literacy barrier.

Regardless of the student or the teacher, you will read about learning breakthroughs where hope might have been lost had the teacher not realized a connection while at the same time exhibiting patience and understanding and the ability to see and move beyond the lesson plans. As I'm sure you will note, the teachers often spend a great deal of time reflecting on the students prior to initiating an instructional response. You may want to ask yourself questions while you read, keeping detailed thoughts in the margins of the book. For example, "What made this teacher try this particular instructional method or approach?"

Expecting the *Aha!* Moment

Karen Kindle

I had been waiting *for the moment,
but had stopped* expecting *it.*

*Waiting is passive. Working with
struggling readers and writers is draining,
emotionally and physically.*

WE'VE ALL SEEN IT—THAT INCREDIBLE MOMENT in teaching when a student finally gets it. That *Aha!* moment, when the light comes on and you know it all makes sense. As teachers, we live for *Ahas*. They energize and excite us. They remind us why we have chosen to spend our days with other people's children and our nights and weekends in endless preparation.

Sometimes we wait a long time to see that look of dawning comprehension. Surely, we think, it should have come by now. This was a good lesson—it worked great last year. Then there comes a point when even the most patient, dedicated teacher can't help thinking . . .

Maybe this child just can't do it.

Everyone at my school had decided that "Sasha" just couldn't do it. I knew all about her before she ever entered my ESL classroom; she was a frequent topic of discussion in the lounge. Sasha entered school in first grade speaking no English. Even after a year in school, she could not respond orally to simple questions. She was still unable to identify most of the letters in the alphabet. So Sasha repeated first grade. She made good progress the second time around, but everyone tends to forget how far a student has come, and look only at how far she still has to go. Her classroom teacher wanted to make a referral for special education, but Sasha's limited English would invalidate the testing and the district did not have the means to test her in her home language.

Then there comes a point when even the most patient, dedicated teacher can't help thinking . . . Maybe this child just can't do it.

Sasha came to me for her ELA block—ninety minutes every day. It was hard to remain patient with her at times. She did everything so much slower than everyone else. During our reading lesson toward the end of the morning, she would raise her hand to answer a question from the early morning warm-up activity. Her comments and questions were hard to understand since they were so out of context and her vocabulary was so limited.

On one particular morning, I had a great lesson prepared. We were working on the silent *e* spelling pattern using plastic letters as manipulatives. It was a fun lesson and the students were completely engaged:

Make the word *cap*. Now add the magic *e*, wave your hand and say abracadabra! Cap is now _____.

And the children would shout *CAPE!*

A bit corny, but it was working. I have no idea how many examples we did. The kids were doing great. Even Sasha seemed to be keeping up with us, making the words, and adding the magic *e* and even calling out the new word—although just a hair behind everyone else. I patted myself on the back.

A good lesson. Ready to move on to the next step.

We did a few more examples as I gathered the things I needed to transition to the next activity.

And then it happened. *"OH, OH, OH!"* Sasha jumped out of her seat. I will never forget the look on her face as she finally had her *Aha!* moment. Her face lit up and her eyes were sparkling. *"Oh, the e—when you make word—the e—nother word!"* Aha! Sasha and I quickly went through more and more examples. She could hardly contain her excitement. She finally understood what we were doing, and how the spelling pattern related to the sound of the words.

Children are not the only ones who have *Aha!* moments. Sasha led me to experience my own. When I didn't think I could stand one more magic *e* word, Sasha was just getting to the place where she had enough practice that she could grasp the concept. I had been *waiting* for the moment, but had stopped *expecting* it.

Waiting is passive. Working with struggling readers and writers is draining, emotionally and physically. We wait and wonder. It is hard to keep that unbidden thought—the idea that they will *never* get it—from entering your consciousness. That is when expecting success becomes even more critical.

Reaching Struggling Students

Expecting is active. Model one more time. Complete more examples. Find yet another way to explain it. Expect it. And then be ever vigilant, always on the lookout for that spark, that look of surprise when you know it happened—Aha!

In today's diverse classrooms it is more difficult and more important than ever for the teacher to really know the students well. Assessments help us to know each student's strengths and weaknesses in the core components of reading, but they will not tell us how to reach the student who is struggling to grasp these important concepts. Effective teaching means looking beyond the numbers to the child, learning what types of activities engage and motivate, and finding the right match between student and method. Most important, effective teaching means expecting success.

Facing My Chair Forward

Limor Pinhasi-Vittorio

People begin life as motivated learners, not as passive beings. Children naturally join the world around them. They learn by interacting, by experimenting. . . . Language intrigues children; they have needs they want met; they busy the older people in their lives with questions and requests for show me, tell me.

—SHOR, 1992; P. 17

AS A LITERACY SPECIALIST AND TEACHER EDUCATOR, I find myself reflecting back to my earlier experiences as a teacher in the public school system in the United States and in Israel. Every year and every student I have taught have become significant to me as I continue to learn from all my students and from every experience. However, of all my years of teaching, I remember the first class I taught in America most clearly. Upon completing my master's degree in special education, I was full of ambition and motivation to teach where I felt I was needed most. Hence, I pursued

11

my teaching in one of the rather poorer neighborhoods of a U.S. metropolitan area. I was assigned to teach in a third-grade classroom with students who were categorized as emotionally disturbed children.

During the initial orientation, I shared my excitement to work with the students assigned to my class with the principal, along with my future plans for promoting their success in school. The principal looked at me and with a sarcastic smile said that I should not be concerned about literacy since the most significant task was "to prevent the students from jumping out of the windows." Those words were like a splash of cold water on my face, and yet I *knew* that every child can learn and that it is our right, and particularly our human right, to learn to read.

Those words were like a splash of cold water on my face, and yet I knew *that every child can learn and that it is our right, and particularly our human right, to learn to read.*

During the first month of teaching, I learned that most of the students could not read at their grade level at all, and the two that could at least decode on grade level were unable to comprehend what they read. But it turned out that they could learn. I could tell many stories of success from that first year, but here I focus on one eight-year-old boy, "Markus."

Markus could not identify the letters nor did he know their sounds. His attitude toward me and school was usually one of anger, occasionally moderating to indifference (Kohl, 1995). He refused to face the front of the class. He would put his head down or instigate a fight with other students every time we attempted to read or write, and he would spit and curse at other students as well as at me. During my first few months in the classroom, I focused on building a mutual trust between us. I was aware that the only way that success and learning could enter into this space was if Markus and the rest of the students felt safe in the classroom (Paley, 1997; Shor, 1992).

Gradually, our classroom became Markus's safe haven. We built a Reading Center where I brought in a beautiful quilt, which we spread on the floor and covered with nice pillows. Markus himself accessorized the Center and, with encouragement and acknowledgment of his offerings, drew pictures and signs that would go well there. By contributing to the development of the Reading Center and the classroom at large, Markus found a way to embrace the classroom space and in particular the Reading Center as his own place (Shor, 1992).

Since Markus could not identify letters or their sounds, I asked him to become my assistant as I created a letter card-game. Together we thought of how we would like the game to be developed; eventually we decided that the goal of the game would be to find the appropriate letter for the word that described the picture. Markus initially focused on the coloring of the picture. After a few days he wanted to draw the picture, and by the end of the week he actually wrote the letters on the cards. Throughout the first week he played the card game and at the same time he took the role of the teacher. He guided the rest of the students on the directions of how to play this game—this game over which he had developed a sense of ownership. His ability to recognize the letters and their sounds grew as he built upon his successes. Creating the card game was a next step in promoting his literacy skills.

What had happened was that while we developed our classroom community and the Reading Center, the sense of safety in the class was building as well. Markus allowed himself to learn; he did not resist the learning (Kohl, 1995). Moreover, I found out that learning occurred when the task was relevant and of interest to him. Aware of the importance of incorporating Markus's interest in the literacy activities, I provided him and all the other children in the class with writing journals. This journal was different from other notebooks. Markus, like the others in the class, was allowed to write or draw anything he wanted to share with me. I did not force him to write at all (Elbow, 1998). Indeed at first, Markus would only draw a picture. As time went on, the pictures became more elaborate as he attempted to convey his thoughts; he even created a collage as he attempted to communicate more clearly with me.

After every entry Markus and I would sit together "to read" what he had expressed through the drawing. As he read, I precisely wrote what he had just said. While I was modeling writing, I noticed that Markus was curious about how I was writing. Gradually, Markus's entries included more letters; he used his knowledge from the card game and he gathered the courage to construct words and later on, sentences. The most amazing part in this process occurred when Markus took complete ownership for his own learning, when *he* directed my teaching. He asked how to make certain sounds—curious and motivated to enhance his own learning process. The motivation to learn was internal.

At the end of the school year, Markus was excelling in class. His rapid academic progression led to an immense improvement in his behavior, and he was recommended to be mainstreamed. Reflecting upon Markus's learning success I can confidently say that it was not only one factor that promoted his success but rather a combination of many. First, creating a safe environment was fundamental in promoting his learning. Second, as his teacher, I was tuned in to his learning styles as well as able to engage his interest in a supportive and nonthreatening manner. Finally, I believed in him and allowed him the space to grow based on his own individuality and learning style. These factors, as well as the sense of community that developed in the classroom, permitted learning where Markus, the learner, took ownership for his own learning.

One Who Learns Differently from the Rest

Now as a teacher-educator I find the story of Markus extremely important and inspiring for literacy educators. In every classroom, teachers can find a "Markus" who learns differently from the rest and gains confidence initially in a distinct style of learning (Leland, Harste, & Helt, 2000). As teachers, we strive to provide all our students with the optimum way of learning; we can tap into their interests and allow them to grow and develop up to their own potential. The words of Auerbach and Wallerstein echo in my mind: "Our role as teachers is to create a safe environment [where] students can express opinions and most importantly, generate their own language materials for learning and peer teaching" (1987, p. vii).

Books Will Be Her Legs

Vicki S. Collet

*To acquire the habit of reading is to construct
for yourself a refuge from almost all the
miseries of life.*

—W. SOMERSET MAUGHAM

THERE ARE MANY WAYS TO MEASURE SUCCESS in education. For me,
success has a face in one child's smile. When I first met "Angela,"
she was a spunky little three-year-old, running uninhibited
around the yard of her new neighbor while her parents stopped
to chat. Now it's that spunkiness that keeps nine-year-old
Angela out of her wheelchair most of the time.

I remember the call we got on Christmas Eve when Angela
was five. Friends were asked to pray for Angela, who wasn't
expected to make it through the night. Angela had slipped into a
diabetic coma and suffered heart trauma and a stroke all in one
bout. She stubbornly clung to life, however, in spite of continuing
health concerns. Two years later, finally getting to the root of all
her physical ails, doctors diagnosed Angela with a genetic
degenerative disease—one that will steal first her mobility, then
her voice, and finally her life.

Last year, Angela came to my school. She'd been in private school, but her need for special education services brought the family to the doors of a public institution that could better meet her needs. Because of the brain injury caused by Angela's stroke, she had struggled to learn to read. When she enrolled in my school, she was a nine-year-old repeating third grade and reading at the pre-primer level. I had the chance to work with her all year in a one-on-one setting, meeting twice a week before school.

I was determined to help her acquire the gift of reading—a gift that I hoped would lift her beyond the limitations of her failing body to explore new and imagined worlds and learn about things she'd never see or do.

During our half-hour sessions together, our approach included multisensory activities that overcame the limitations of her brain injury. We used mirrors so that she could see how the sounds were formed and colored tiles to manipulate as we built phonemic awareness. We contrasted similar sounds and compared vowel patterns with the same sound. We took word sorts one step further by color-coding the patterns she discovered. I taught her using a framework and sequence that helped her organize this information in her brain so that it would be easy to retrieve while reading. Angela learned to recognize small words automatically and to take long words apart. She already had a sizable vocabulary and good thinking skills; what she needed were keys to help her break the code. As she learned these keys, we read great stories together so that she could apply what she was learning. Our first chapter book together was *The Courage of Sarah Noble,* whose main character was as spunky as Angela. Before long, however, she was reading more difficult books like *Because of Winn Dixie* on her own.

I was determined to help her acquire the gift of reading—a gift that I hoped would lift her beyond the limitations of her failing body to explore new and imagined worlds and learn about things she'd never see or do. Angela and I worked with dogged determination. Her family was supporting her at every side as she made rapid advances into the world of readers.

Literacy Will Provide an Important Freedom

By the end of third grade, she had a voracious reading appetite, consuming chapter books at an amazing rate! Every time I saw her, she updated me on the books she had finished since our last meeting. She was finding joy in imagined worlds. I believe the books gave her halting legs wings, and I know that as the disease takes its toll (and Angela's reading ability continues to increase!) literacy will provide an important freedom for this persistent, delightful child.

Thinking of Angela brings the value of literacy into clearer focus for me. Angela's story shows what I believe to be a universal value of literacy: it is liberating! When we read, we walk without feet and fly without wings.

"I Guess Kids Can Be Teachers Sometimes"

Cynthia J. Poston

Though we search the world over for the beautiful,
we find it within or we find it not.

—RALPH WALDO EMERSON

I WAS A READING SPECIALIST AND LITERACY COACH at the elementary level in a large suburban public school district. In that role, I spent time daily with students at various grade levels. In one third-grade classroom, I met "Ahmed," who had moved with his parents and siblings to the United States from Pakistan. Ahmed was polite but reserved, rarely sharing his writing pieces during the Author's Chair portion of writers' workshop. His thoughtful brown eyes seemed to miss nothing, yet often the school day would pass without Ahmed sharing his thoughts with his classmates or teachers.

As the students were busily writing independently one day during writers' workshop, I took the opportunity to confer with Ahmed, hoping this might provide a more comfortable opportunity for him to share some of his writing with me. I firmly believed, and still do, that the foundation of good teaching is a trusting relationship between student and teacher, and thought this might be a beginning for me and Ahmed. I was soon to find out that this trusting relationship between students and teachers is not only a foundation but perhaps the most critical step toward learning—not just on Ahmed's part, in this case, but mine as well.

I approached Ahmed as he was writing and noticed that he had begun, as the classroom teacher had suggested in mini-lessons, to organize his thoughts on a story web. At the center of his web, he had written "Eid." Out to the side, he had drawn lines to connect details such as "fasting" and "celebration." After commenting on how focused he seemed in getting his ideas down on paper, I asked Ahmed what he could tell me about Eid, hoping we might discover more details to include in his rough draft.

I concluded the conference by commenting as I often do after conferring with students, "Thanks for sharing your ideas with me today." Then I was compelled to add, "You really taught me a lot today."

Not having much personal knowledge of the holiday Ahmed was writing about, Eid (or more precisely *Eid ul-Fitr* according to the Muslim religion), I asked Ahmed to please "teach me" about how his family observed this special day. I soon learned, through Ahmed's animated and enthusiastic account of this important day in his life, that Eid marked the end of Ramadan, which meant the end of a month-long period of fasting for Muslims. I still am unsure if the source of his excitement was devotion or relief, but his obvious delight in writing about Eid told me that this was a topic worth exploring.

We continued our conversation, with Ahmed giving a detailed account of how he, his siblings, and his parents observed Ramadan and Eid. Ahmed not only taught me about his family's beliefs and practices, he also showed me his relationships with his extended family living in Pakistan—cousins, uncles, aunts, and grandparents who all shared his enthusiasm for Eid and who, according to Ahmed, missed him as much as he missed them. During this brief but powerful encounter, I learned as much about Ahmed as an individual as I did about the Muslim religion.

I concluded the conference by commenting as I often do after conferring with students, "Thanks for sharing your ideas with me today." Then I was compelled to add, "You really taught me a lot today."

Ahmed smiled broadly and returned to his story web, anxiously jotting down ideas before they were forever lost. I continued circulating to other students in the room, dropping in and conferring as I went.

A few weeks later, the third-grade classes began a unit on letter writing. As an authentic purpose for writing, the third graders wrote an actual letter to a person of their choice. In my school mailbox, I found a short but moving letter written in Ahmed's best third-grade handwriting:

Dear Ms. Poston,
I didn't know that I could teach you so much about Eid.
I guess kids can be teachers sometimes, too.

Yours truly,
Ahmed

After that, Ahmed and I made a point of greeting one another in the hallways and on the playground. His classroom teacher began to notice a tentative willingness to share his writing pieces during Author's Chair. Although Ahmed was still quiet and reserved by nature, he soon was teaching his classmates about his life in the Muslim community, and aspects of the life and culture he experienced in Pakistan. He had much to teach all of us, if we just took a moment to listen.

Willing to Share

Through my work with Ahmed, I realized that empowering students to teach us, and being willing to accept their wisdom, is perhaps the first, most necessary step toward building those crucial personal relationships. Ahmed's framed letter hangs near my desk, reminding me daily of this important lesson—taught to me by a third grader who was willing to share a bit of himself with me.

Through the Red Door of Room 207
Angie Zapata

*By listening attentively, giving children full
attention, the teacher indicates that what they have
to say is important—that they have expertise that is
of value. When she asks questions, it is in order
to be further informed, not to check that the child's
answer is in conformity with her knowledge about
the topic. And by inviting other children to listen
and ask questions in the same way, she builds
up in each child a feeling of self-respect and
confidences in what he or she knows and can do
and, at the same time, a feeling of respect for
others as well.*

—GORDON WELLS, THE MEANING MAKERS

"HENRY" DRIFTED QUIETLY THROUGH THE RED DOOR OF ROOM 207
on the first day of third grade. With his right hand, he tightly
clutched his mother's dress as the index finger of his left hand

found a comfortable spot in his mouth. Henry's eyes were closed, and he trailed behind her in the same way a baby elephant clings to its mother's tail.

His mother greeted me with a warm smile. And as she graciously shook my hand, Henry opened his eyes, peeked up at me, and smiled that smile that I would come to know so well. In moments, he hid behind his mother's dress, eyes closed and index finger finding its way into his mouth once again. By the last day of third grade, Henry would compellingly reveal the wealth of knowing, strength, and wit he had within. But this would be the one occasion I would remember Henry as reticent, and it was the first of many times Henry would walk through the red door of room 207.

If I did not get the message fast enough, he would then bury his head between his arms on his desk, occasionally glancing at me to see if I bought his act. Admittedly, time and again I felt at a loss in these moments.

I came to know Henry's personal history. It was a story of loss and reconnection with his mother after a six-year absence. Since kindergarten, he had been enrolled in five different elementary schools. Making a home with his mother was to be a fresh start for the two of them in every way imaginable. The dream was abruptly interrupted by another separation from his mother after our fourth week of school. By the sixth week of school, Henry was gone and did not return for another month. He was shuffled from shelter to shelter, aunt to uncle, and finally returned to his father and grandmother in Austin. Henry's eyes were heavy with hurt and disappointment when he returned through the red door of room 207.

CONNECTION

Depending on how much sleep he had the night before or if he had breakfast, Henry regularly found a place in the principal's office for some indiscretion on the bus or the playground or with his special education teacher. I initially worried about how I might best support Henry's ways of knowing and social position in a room of third graders. He was an emergent reader eager to tickle people with his words, ready to show that he could write his first name as well as part of his last name, and keen to let any other student know if he did not agree. Yet despite what would appear to be an obvious mismatch for a student and a classroom, my concerns faded as Henry promptly created his space in the classroom. He was an artist and a powerful kickball player, a comedian and a loyal friend—all invaluable commodities in the world of eight-year-olds. And although some days felt longer than others for Henry, he soon became the first student in the mornings to run through the red door of room 207.

Henry showed me that /l/ and /e/ were the two phonemes firmly fixed in his alphabet goodie bag. So we began with what he knew. We boogied to *Chicka Chicka Boom Boom*, tracing letters in the air, in the rice, creating them on the computer. We listened to *What a Wonderful World* on the iPod as we followed along in the book. We made tiny pattern books about the foods he loved, the people in his life, the animals he heard, and the friends he had. We wrote thank-you notes to his beloved university buddy and the adored pre-K class he visited daily as a third-grade buddy. Although he had perfected the art of guessing the word, he counted on a good picture walk to get things going. We read aloud favorite books again and again, talking back to characters. He charged Edmund with selfishness for betraying his brother and sisters to the White Witch and notified Henry Green he was just crazy for eating all of that chocolate.

Each day, I had to be ready with a variety of invitations and activities, for Henry was quick to let me know when reading and

Through the Red Door of Room 207

writing had outworn their welcome. He had a way of rolling his eyes to the very back of his head so that only white could be seen between his fluttering eyelashes. If I did not get the message fast enough, he would then bury his head between his arms on his desk, occasionally glancing at me to see if I bought his act. Admittedly, time and again I felt at a loss in these moments. But I soon learned that more often than not, the "just right" book or the "just right hug" or the "just right" marker could turn things around. Every day we did something new. Every day we celebrated his unique insights and what his latest discoveries were. Every day offered another lifelong lesson for both of us to take home after leaving the red door of room 207.

We all spent the same amount of time in third grade, but it was Henry who traveled the furthest as a learner and as a teacher. He transformed *Little Red Riding Hood* into *Little Red in the Hood*, with Fifty Cent as the villain. On the last day of third grade, he left with a backpack stuffed with art supplies and books as well as an armful of pictures, memory books, and a class DVD. As we sang our good-bye song, Henry peeked up at me, dropped all of his things on the floor and gave me a hug. When it was over he let his smile light up his eyes, picked up his treasures, and skipped out the red door of room 207.

A Place to Begin and a Place to Go

Henry taught me how each of us, no matter our age, has a place to begin and places to go. He taught me how far a kind invitation to learn can take you, the importance of humility, and how strong a nine-year-old can be in the face of heartbreaking odds. His ways of knowing and hard work culminated in a publication of his very own.

To Know Them Is to Teach Them

Martha Ford

Find out who they are and what has happened
in their lives.

I ENTER THE EIGHTH-GRADE WRITING CLASS. *The students are barely under control, but I know what to do. I have been at this for a long time. I believe in these children and hope they will believe in me before we are done. Later, when we discuss today's lesson, I will tell the teacher how to rearrange their seats.*

"Tomas" waits for me, just like many before him and most likely after him. Sometimes male; sometimes female. He deliberately tilts his head to the side, the eyes staring at me, a small smile on his face. He is already drawing before I even introduce myself, just to let me know who is in charge. He will see.

I tell a story about the beach, using the inverted triangle to model the writer's thinking process. I sketch, dance with the words, and make eighth graders laugh. I talk about being a grandma, and now everyone is with me. You cannot help but smile at a grandmother.

The novice teacher has asked for help with getting her students to write. This of course is my favorite thing to do. It is really quite easy but very hard at the same time. You have to believe that it will happen and then show young writers how to make it happen. If they are to become writers, they must write. And what do they know better than their own personal stories, shared histories, dreams, beliefs? These are the universal themes that bind us in our humanity.

When I am done modeling, I ask the essential question: What is my story really about? The writers talk about family, relationships, mothers and sons, grandchildren, risk taking, and the worrying of a grandmother. While the writers record some ideas that result from the conversation, I walk over to Tomas. He is still drawing.

Never intrude upon the identity of the children with whom we work. Give them space. Find out who they are and what has happened in their lives, good and bad, unusual and ordinary, important or quotidian.

"I see you are an artist. Perhaps you will illustrate your story. Who taught you to draw?"

"My brother."

"That will make a good story."

Then I notice his shirt. I see a photo of him with a boy who looks like him. Startled, I know that the older boy is dead without actually reading the words on the shirt.

"You have other stories to tell, too."

Give Them Space

During the follow-up session the teacher explains that the young man in the photograph was murdered a week earlier: our young writer witnessed the death of his brother. Once again, I am grateful for what I have learned so far about teaching. Never intrude upon the identity of the children with whom we work. Give them space. Find out who they are and what has happened in their lives, good and bad, unusual and ordinary, important or quotidian. Conversation and the writing process give us a glimpse into their worlds. Once they understand that we respect and celebrate their stories, perhaps they will listen to ours.

I must move on to another class. As I leave, Tomas starts to write.

Reflections on the Breakthroughs

Susan E. Israel

WHAT I THOUGHT I WOULD FIND WHEN REREADING the stories for this section would be accounts by teachers whose goal was to show how to get students to read and write. What I discovered were stories about how the teachers learned something different about their instructional habits and how they revised their instruction to enable a literacy connection according to what they learned from their students. One way I have changed my thinking is that I've learned that students like to celebrate small accomplishments—the small literacy accomplishments they make on a daily basis. To them it is the little barriers that cause them a momentary collapse of mind, or of heart. "Get me past that one little barrier," is what I hear the students saying to the teacher, "and soon I can conquer the bigger barriers, one by one. Guess what that means, teacher?"

What I found interesting in these stories is the way the authors never gave up on their students. Regardless of the student's age or degree of ability, they kept on trying. A change of instructional goal took place with the teachers first before they were able to discover a way to observe any noticeable successes. When things were not going well for them, and to me that means, when they were frustrated with their teaching because they still could not reach their students, they stepped back and took time to reflect. What they realized was that their first successes were not in the form of measurable gains but in behaviors. Getting to know the students became the foundational strategy before learning took place. As Limor Pinhasi-Vittorio concludes in her breakthrough, learning took place when it was relevant. "As teachers, we strive to provide all our students with the optimum way of learning; we can tap into their interests and allow them to grow and develop up to their own potential." What I found relevant to me in the lessons teachers learned was that teachers should allow students to learn in their own way and that teachers should help children gain confidence in their own style of learning first. This requires teachers to really get to know the students.

In reviewing these stories where teaching practices helped students, I have come to realize that an important aspect of teaching is the ability of the teacher to notice when something in the teaching process is not working, and to take a few steps backward to get to know the child and find a way to move forward and change instruction when things were not going as planned.

The teacher's willingness to learn from the student creates an environment that fosters a trusting relationship. Once this is established, students feel safer about allowing teachers to get to know them. The result, as demonstrated in the stories, is that the students make a significant breakthrough in reading or writing at the micro-learning level, which leads to focused gains in achievement overall.

Breakthrough Elements

The importance of getting to know students comes through in these stories. Although the process for knowing the students differs for each teacher, the teachers often started with observations, went through a process of reflection in correspondence with their knowledge of the child, and then used this simple assessment to guide their thinking about the appropriate learning approach for their at-risk student. What is consistent in the stories is the message of how students helped teachers learn what matters, what helps students, and that requires getting to know them, building trust, and allowing students to begin their literacy transformation at their own learning point and not within the confines of the teacher's lesson plan. What is also evident in the stories is the way humility plays a role in the teacher's decision to make a behavioral or instructional change. I could hear the teachers' thoughts as I read their stories: *"I need to listen to these kids. What I am doing is not working. What is it I need to do to help this child* today?" Teachers placed value on the amount of time it took to learn about the places the children had been and the places they wanted to go. The teachers came to realize that regardless of the child or the learning situation, a foundation of good teaching is building a trusting relationship. Teachers who realized this also realized that the waiting was worth it; that perseverance and patience pay off, too.

REFLECTION QUESTIONS

- What is most important to this child that I need to know before learning can occur?
- When is it appropriate for a teacher to allow children space to learn in their own way? Should teachers allow space before or after necessary skills have been taught?
- What do you think "we have places to begin and places to go" means relative to a specific student you wish to help?
- What can you learn from the student you are trying to help that will assist you in moving beyond the literacy barrier?

- What do you know about the students you are trying to help to increase learning?
- Do you believe a struggling reader or writer might actually be a very good reader or writer who is simply waiting for the brain to make a new connection so the moment of learning can occur?

Lessons Learned

In summary, I see several lessons in the stories in Part One. First of all, we should create safe havens in the classroom so students can learn and want to learn. We should begin where each student is instructionally, work together with the student to create a literacy plan, and always be on the lookout for teachable moments. We can support children who have trouble reading English by dictating stories that they tell and transcribing them so they can learn to read words in English. We should allow children opportunities to generate writing ideas that are meaningful to them rather than imposing writing topics upon them. We can use words that students use when writing and allow students to learn how to read from their own personal vocabulary lists. Simply put, another way to look at breakthrough moments is to look for ways to overcome learning barriers for students. Perhaps you know a child or are currently working with a child like Sasha, who struggled with identifying letters in the alphabet because of her own English language barriers; like Markus, who was reading below grade level and unable to find a way to match sounds with letters, or like Angela, who was almost forgotten in a special education curriculum that did not help her find a way to organize information in her brain. Think about these children, and you will learn what they are trying to tell you is, "Teacher, keep trying, do not give up on me and stop believing. Together, we can find my way to literacy."

Ten Literacy Breakthrough Actions You Can Take Today

1. Make a list of the students you need to help today.
2. Make a list of the top five things you know about each of these students.
3. Write down five questions you still have about each student and think about how this information might help you with a literacy breakthrough.
4. Describe your teaching environment. How would your students describe your teaching environment relative to their learning needs?
5. Make a list of what each student needs from you today to be successful today.
6. If your student most in need struggles with emotional issues that hinder learning, invite your school psychologist to share some ideas that will enable you to better help this student.
7. Invite your students with limited vocabulary to make their own books of all the words they do know. Use that word list to teach synonyms and antonyms, which will enhance their vocabulary and teach them more words and word relationships.
8. Set literacy goals for the students you are working with and discuss them together.
9. Think about what moment you are waiting for relative to the student you are helping. What would be a literacy breakthrough? Once you have thought about what it is you are waiting for, write it down and ask

Reflections on the Breakthroughs

yourself, Why is this important to me? Is this important to the child?

10. Celebrate the next literacy breakthrough moment by making a home call to a parent or guardian.

Further Reading

When you need a read-aloud to help foster trusting environments: *The Dot* by Peter Reynolds (Cambridge, Mass.: Candlewick Press, 2004) is a story about an art teacher who framed one of her students' work and hung it over her desk, even though he did not think his work was valuable. The picture was a picture of a dot signed by the student. It was his best work at the time and she demonstrated how she valued his work no matter what. The story continues to highlight the boy's inspirational moment to develop further art-dot-related masterpieces. Lots of lessons on respect can be learned from this book.

    When you need a professional development resource to help you think about and know your students: *Motivating Primary-Grade Students (Solving Problems in Teaching of Literacy)* by Michael Pressley, Sara E. Dolezal Kersey, Lisa Raphael Bogaert, Lindsey Mohan, Alysia D. Roehrig, and Kristen Bogner Warzon (New York: Guilford Press, 2003) will help you think differently and continue to transform your thinking about what it means to help someone learn to read and write. This volume provides lots of research-based ideas on what motivates students. The authors also discuss demotivating actions that discourage learning, and they offer many lists of factors that will help you reach students and build caring environments that will motivate students to learn to read. In addition, the case studies written by exemplary teachers from the study provide a variety of practical suggestions. Parents will also benefit from reading this book or obtaining the motivating lists referenced throughout the book.

When either you or your students need to hear a story that comes from the heart: *See the Ocean* by Estelle Condra, illustrated by Linda Crockett-Blassingame (Nashville, Tenn.: Eager Minds Press, 1994). Have you seen the ocean? This is a question you can ask your children before you read this book. Ask them to describe the ocean and have them list all the things they like about it. Now ask them to try to think of all the different ways they could see the ocean or learn about the ocean. Now you can read this moving story about a girl who can only see the ocean through her heart.

When you want to learn about how to inspire students to want to learn: *Activating the Desire to Learn* by Bob Sullo (Alexandria, Va.: ASCD, 2007) is a practitioner-oriented book that offers practical ideas that teachers can implement today. The methods and instructional intervention ideas discussed can easily be modified for any classroom.

PART TWO

Motivation

THE RIGHT
BOOK CAN MAKE
A DIFFERENCE

About the Stories

Susan E. Israel

THE POWER OF BOOKS AND LITERATURE—including unusual books, favorite books, and other types of texts—to excite and engage students is a leading theme in the Part Two stories. The power of choice is also important when it comes to helping children develop increased literacy skills. Choice works hand-in-hand with the concept of personalization. Just as I choose what to read, I also like to personalize my content so that it has reading value to me.

One day while I was working on this book, I read the *Wall Street Journal*'s Weekly Journal Section, which usually includes one or more book reviews. I enjoy reading the book reviews because I like to learn about new books being published and I also value book recommendations by experts. Reading book reviews from the *WSJ* helps me realize what is going on in the publishing world outside education. I enjoy staying abreast of popular books or new markets and genres. Reading the book reviews helps me find books that I am interested in learning more about and how other content, which I probably wouldn't know about if I did not read the reviews, might make a difference in the world of education. One book that I recently checked out of the library because of the recommendation in the *Wall*

Street Journal was *The Dumbest Generation: How the Digital Age Stupefies Young Americans and Jeopardizes Our Future.* As a literacy professional, I was curious as to why the author, Mark Bauerlein, titled his book as he did. What can I learn from his book that might help me understand learning characteristics of today's students? What would reading this book do to my own thinking about reading and writing? Personalizing book selections has a lot to do with interest, although it is not the only element. I asked myself what will I gain in knowledge value from reading *The Dumbest Generation?* What do I value?

Understanding our own habits of book selection can also help us be better teachers and literacy professionals. Our criteria for book selection might not be to read about current events or learn about popular genres but to explore personal interests that we may have. The stories in this part demonstrate that children also like to have some say in what they are reading, which allows them to create a personal and meaningful connection.

The stories in Part Two communicate the message that knowing the student will help you in selecting the right book, a key motivational factor when working to strengthen students' reading and writing skills. The teachers in this part may not describe themselves as experts but are well qualified and experienced educators who have worked with children at varying ability levels. The students are described as being uninterested in reading, reluctant readers and writers, special education students, students with language-based learning disabilities, and readers who do not want to read.

The stories center on literacy breakthroughs achieved in large part as a result of particular books or literature that made a difference in the way the teachers approached their lessons or viewed their students. The opening story, written by Danna Parsons, describes how Dillon, a reluctant first grader who struggles to pay attention, became motivated to like reading by listening to a humorous chapter book. Emily Manning, who shares a love of Dr. Seuss (a near-universal childhood favorite), talks about how reading *The Lorax* to her second graders inspired the entire class to embark on a special project. Elizabeth Frye describes how a certain type of book helps motivate her third-grade class to write stories and view themselves as authors. Karen Jorgensen, faced with helping a struggling bilingual student prepare for an English medium school, shows how a particular book helped motivate the child to overcome his reluctance and engage in reading. William Bintz and Pamela Wright coauthor a description of the unique meaning a special needs student finds in a story and how the class responds. Kathy Egawa, a tutor and literacy coach, describes the steps she took to help a fourth grader with diagnosed reading disabilities make impressive strides in reading comprehension. Lindsay Grow describes the powerful writing generated by her fifth-grade class after they were inspired by a particular poet. Lisa Janes offers a story about how one of her fifth-grade students, a boy, brings a book of questionable literary merit to class and the excitement it generates for his classmates. Part Two concludes with a story by Daniel Holm, who taught in England for a year and talks about the importance of sharing with students books that have personal meaning.

Carpet Fuzz, a Staple, and a Story

Danna Parsons

There is more treasure in books than in all
the pirates' loot on Treasure Island.

—Walt Disney

"DILLON" DID NOT WALK, HE BOUNCED. I always thought that if I had one ounce of Dillon's energy I could wrangle twenty-one first graders every day on one cup of coffee instead of three. No, there was never a doubt that Dillon was spirited. He sprinted to be first in line; he twisted and turned in the hallway on the way to lunch; he rolled on the carpet during share time. Everything Dillon did was fueled by an immense amount of energy. Everything, that is, except reading.

When it came time to read, Dillon deflated. When summoned to the table for reading group he was in no hurry. Browsing the centers where the other students worked, strolling by the window to gaze outside, Dillon always chose the scenic route to the reading table. His participation during reading group mirrored the same unenthusiastic manner in which he arrived. Whereas he eagerly shouted answers during class discussions, whether called on or not, he mumbled when asked to read a word on a page. His hands were rarely still throughout the day, but when asked to follow along with his finger, his hand remained quiet, lingering haphazardly on the page.

With clear signs of a bright boy who liked to learn, I knew I needed to find the spark that would kindle the flame of the joy of reading.

Dillon's lack of interest in reading was not exclusive to reading group. Read-aloud time prompted different behaviors from those of the deflated Dillon. During read-aloud Dillon became a discoverer. While the other students sat attentively, laughing or oohhing and aahhing as the story unfolded, Dillon used this time to discover the world around him. Sitting on the carpet was a new adventure with each visit. On one occasion, he picked and twirled on the carpet, collecting the fuzz in his palm as if unearthing sacred gold coins. Another time, he bent and molded a discarded staple into a tool to rub etchings in the bottom of his shoe. Carpet fuzz, a staple, a ripped seam on the cuff of his jeans, all these trivial things captured Dillon's attention, leaving little if any for the book being shared.

The problem was not Dillon's inability to read; for a beginning first grader, this is not uncommon. Instead, he did not seem to *want* to read. He simply was not interested. With clear signs of a bright boy who liked to learn, I knew I needed to find the spark that would kindle the flame of the joy of reading in Dillon.

After several weeks of sharing picture books for read-aloud time, I decided to begin reading a short chapter book. I chose this chapter book with Dillon specifically in mind. The main character was a little girl who, just like Dillon, was a free spirit full of spunky determination.

The afternoon I began the book was unlike any other. Dillon had found a new treasure on the carpet, one that even the most attentive student might find irresistible: a small piece of the blue sticky putty that was used to tack posters to the wall. As I began to read, assigning the main character an innocent but feisty voice that drew laughs from the class immediately, I stole a glance at Dillon. He watched, smiling slightly as he continued to roll the putty round and round in his fingers. I knew that any moment that putty could secure his attention as closely as it had once secured a poster to the wall. I continued, reading with gusto, animating the characters with facial expressions and intonation. Then as the first chapter drew to a close and I nestled the bookmark in the seam, someone at the back of the group called, "*No! Don't stop!*" Such an outburst might seem to deserve a frown, but I smiled from ear to ear as I realized the source of the eruption. . . .

Dillon had discovered a new treasure.

Dillon's plea was shared by all the students, and by Christmas we had read several books in the series. Carpet fuzz and staples no longer held his interest; instead Dillon brought his own treasures— a matching copy of each book so that he could follow along. Although reading group never made it onto his top ten list of favorite things in school, he was no longer deflated.

Joys of Reading

A spark had been ignited through one simple book that made Dillon laugh. As the saying goes, *laughter is the best medicine*, and in the case of Dillon, it proved to be the perfect cure for his reading ailment. Encouraging unmotivated readers requires choosing books that reveal the joys of reading. Sharing books that induce laughter helps debunk the "reading is boring" myth held by many students. Humor encourages students to be actively engaged in their reading. It serves as a bridge between the reader and the text.

Think about some of your favorite books, books that have made you laugh. If you have not had a chance to share any of them with students, do so in your next lesson. Provide students an opportunity to read some of their favorite parts from books that have made them laugh. Include joke books and puns in your classroom, too. One way to move from reading to writing is to have students think of funny sentence or story starters that will tap into their creative and humorous side. Here are a few to get students thinking:

- When the puppy tried to jump on the sofa, she missed and . . .
- The funniest thing that I have ever done was . . .
- My teacher made me laugh when . . .
- I laughed when my mom . . .
- My grandpa liked to tell jokes and the one I remember most was . . .

A Plan to Listen

Emily Manning

You're not required to complete the work but neither are you free to desist from it.

—RABBI TARPHON

AT THE TIME OF THIS SUCCESS I was teaching second grade in a Southern elementary school. A teacher's life often seems to revolve around plans: every hour of the day and every content area can be summed up and written into a tidy little lesson plan square. I'm naturally and admittedly a planner, so this part of teaching is something that I love. I get pleasure out of planning my week, gathering the materials, and knowing that when I leave my classroom on Friday everything is ready for me to walk into class on Monday.

But anyone who has ever taught—or been a parent—knows that once kids enter the equation even the best plans can sometimes falter. Plans that looked great on paper all of a sudden seem misguided and completely wrong for your class. Those are the times when you question yourself and spend the rest of the night desperately searching for a new way to reach your students.

Fortunately, you also have those rare times when your plans turn into something else entirely. They take on a life of their own and go in a direction that you never planned for or dreamed that they could go. These are moments that I live for as a teacher.

My moments come when I stop and listen to those small voices in my classroom. These moments come when I allow myself to set aside my lists and plans and respond to my students. My favorite moment came the day that I read *The Lorax* by Dr. Seuss.

I have a picture that I keep in my desk at school.
It's of this class standing around our newly
planted tree. It's a picture of a class that has made
a breakthrough—they accomplished something.

For those of you who have never read *The Lorax*, it's about the Onceler who cuts down all the Truffula Trees to make Thneeds (a product that everyone needs). In doing this, he ruins the environment and only at the end does he realize the impact of his actions. The book ends with the Onceler tossing the very last Truffula Tree seed to a boy, telling him to plant it and saying that if there is just one person who cares a whole awful lot, then something can change.

The students were gathered down on the floor listening to the story. As I finished reading the last page, no one spoke. I should preface this by saying that this class was never silent. They were notorious for talking and in my brief teaching time I had never had a class that was quite so social and as a whole just plain talkative. But now they were silent. Not a sound. Not a peep.

I let the silence sit for a few moments. Soon the talking really started, and I just listened. The class decided that they wanted to be the ones that cared a whole awful lot. They wanted to make a difference. They decided to plant a tree. I decided that this plan was better than anything that I had come up with for the week, and together we made a plan of action.

A Class That Has Made a Breakthrough

We spent the next several months researching trees, finding ways to earn money, contacting all the appropriate people to coordinate the digging of the hole, the arrival of the tree, and at last, the planting of the tree.

I have a picture that I keep in my desk at school. It's of this class standing around our newly planted tree. It's a picture of a class that has made a breakthrough—they accomplished something. This picture is a symbol of taking action and being part of something bigger. I look at this picture every once in a while to remind myself what can happen when I stop and listen to those powerful voices in my classroom.

Every Picture Tells a Story: Supporting Young Authors with Wordless Picture Books

Elizabeth M. Frye

AS A READING EDUCATION FACULTY MEMBER, I was invited to work in a second-grade classroom to assist the teacher with writing instruction in 2005–2006. Shel Silverstein's invitation to spin a yarn is meant for children as much as it is for adults, because children love to tell their stories. How can it be, then, that when we ask children to write their stories, many times we hear, "I don't know what to write or how to write that."

This was the question on my mind when I began working with these second graders and discovered that many of them were reluctant writers, and it did not seem to depend on their reading proficiency. The difficulty seemed to have as much to do with imagining a story as it did with the technical skills of writing one. So I started thinking about ways I could assist children in their story imagining and writing. I developed a process to support young writers through pictures, so that they could *conceive* or *imagine, tell,* and with help, *write* a story—authoring wordless picture books.

In wordless picture books, the story is told entirely through the illustrations. With no written language, the text must be created in the reader's mind. That is, the reader must interpret the pictures personally, giving birth to the text of the story. Because of this quality, wordless picture books have the potential to initiate young writers into the process of story creation, where they will see themselves as authors. The shared writing process I used also assists children in learning the mechanics of writing, which so often prevent them from putting text to a story.

The difficulty seemed to have as much to do with imagining a story as it did with the technical skills of writing one. So I started thinking about ways I could assist children in the story imagining and writing.

I began this process of authoring wordless picture books with nine students of differing reading ability. All nine were considered by the classroom teacher to be "reluctant" writers. I started with the wordless storybook *Picnic* by Emily Arnold McCully, and invited the children to become authors. I explained that, together, we would create the words of the story from the pictures and that I would write the words on chart paper; then I would type the story, they would illustrate the pages, we would publish the book, and finally, they would share it with the kindergartners next door. They were immediately excited; the notion that they would write, illustrate, publish, and share, like real authors, blew them away. And that is exactly what happened.

This project had a tremendous impact on two very different children, "Steven" and "Brittany." Through this process, they gained the confidence they needed to become successful in authoring their own stories. Steven was the highest reader in the class with an amazing vocabulary, but he had trouble conceiving or imagining stories. During an interview, Steven shared the following about writing stories: *"Well, it's just not that easy for me because my brain doesn't work that way. I'm not good at making up stories unless a teacher or somebody gives me help."* The pictures provided the imaginative story that, at that time, Steven had a hard time finding inside himself.

Brittany, on the other hand, had a wonderful imagination, but she had trouble generating words because of her lack of writing mechanics, particularly orthographic (spelling) knowledge. This shared writing framework provided an opportunity for her to offer her ideas and thoughts without the challenge of writing the words. She could see the words being written across the chart paper. After the first day of the project, Brittany asked, *"Am I going to get to be an arthur [her own word] again tomorrow? 'Cause I had fun today and I think I'm a good arthur. Yep, I'm good at this arthur stuff."* She was gaining the confidence she would later need to generate her own writing.

This experience has taught me that authoring wordless picture books provides the necessary scaffold that many students need to confidently begin their own story writing—the pictures really do tell the story. Students experience success in a safe collaborative environment where they view themselves as authors. After the project, I interviewed Brittany and asked her if she considered herself to be an author. She exclaimed, *"Yeah! Because the kids in our group came up with a story that had no words. I mean we can do that! After you do it, I feel like, hey, I can do this, it's no problem 'cause I did it before!"* Picture that success.

"I'm an Amazing Reader!"

Karen A. Jorgensen

---

*There really is nothing I can't read. That's why
I like doing it now. That little boy has wanted
to read since he was six.*

ON A HUMID, MOSQUITO-HUMMING SUMMER DAY in the woods of
Minnesota, between the end of second grade in Norway and the
beginning of third grade in the Netherlands, a young bilingual,
Per, became a reader in two languages. Per, a native speaker of
both English and Norwegian, had been living with his two mul-
tilingual parents in a house overlooking mountains and the
Arctic Ocean. He was painfully shy, unwilling to be different from
his peers, and usually reluctant to engage in literacy in either
language. His school experiences in Norway focused on the well-
being of the whole child.

From my research in his second-grade classroom in March,
I knew that Per had "covered" nineteen of twenty-nine letters
during all of first and second grades. I thought, "How will this
child, who isn't reading or writing in Norwegian, ever be ready
for a British curriculum in an English medium school in a few

months?" It gave me a stomachache, because I had been invited by Per's parents to teach him English literacy in preparation for his third-grade year in the Netherlands. I'd taught elementary readers for nine years, considered myself a competent language and literacy teacher, and was the eternal optimist. Until now. I wondered if I was really up for the task—helping Per become literate in English for his third-grade year—all within twenty-five hours of tutoring.

I'd taught elementary readers for nine years, considered myself a competent language and literacy teacher, and was the eternal optimist. Until now.

Per and I reconnected in a part of his summer home in Minnesota that he named "the classroom." While the environment outside the room was an immersion setting for Americans to learn Norwegian, all things inside our space were chosen to facilitate English literacy. I'd collected crates of books in various genres, award winners from both sides of the Atlantic Ocean. There were stuffed animals, stacks of paper, every imaginable writing tool, and a monthly calendar that would serve as our journal of activities in the tutoring sessions. Now "all I had to do" was take my learning about Per's Norwegian literacy and the related methods that provided his emerging skills and bridge it with English literacy and teaching approaches. I still had the stomachache.

Per and I met for tutoring sessions that lasted anywhere from fifteen to seventy-five minutes for a total of twenty-five hours.

We started each day by listing three to five choices on sticky notes. I recorded suggestions with input from Per and then he prioritized which activities he wanted to do first, second, and third. If we didn't make it through the list, some things moved to the next day and others just fell by the wayside according to his interests and needs, although I had veto power. I considered that the choices needed to balance reading, writing, speaking, listening, and opportunities to discuss similarities and differences between his languages. The tutoring was in English unless Per needed a translation for a word, which I then provided in Norwegian. The activities included much reading aloud, shared writing, laughter, and lots of conversation in English. Per's informal reading inventory in June documented success through the second-grade word list and a first-grade narrative text with 80 percent comprehension. How would these sessions ever get him ready for third grade in an English medium school? I had to think less and act more.

I initially believed that Per needed to have "school language" and content. Then I thought that just getting him to be a reader would be enough. Finally I looked at the minimum that had to happen: to convince, and in some ways coerce, Per to want to read. So I moved to the goal of instilling reading joy and being Per's biggest cheerleader. Little did I know that *Captain Underpants* would unlock Per's future as a reader—and not just in one language but two. Dav Pilkey's story is interspersed with childlike drawings, much humor, and descriptions of life through the eyes of budding cartoonists. Per laughed and laughed and laughed. Soon, without noticing, he took the book from me and started reading aloud and then silently. The next day I met Per at our "classroom" and he announced he'd finished the book! This was the first book of his life that he read independently and comprehended. I know . . . I asked sneaky questions! And as luck or the literacy fates would have it, I had the same volume of *Captain*

Underpants in Norwegian, which he then read that day. What a celebration! While I recognized his spontaneous biliteracy and the gravity of our shared successes, Per simply announced, "I'm an *amazing* reader!"

The rest of our fifteen hours of tutoring flew by, and we did get into content and school language through chemistry experiments, talk shows, writing troll stories, and reading any book that had cartoon-like illustrations or anthropomorphism. Per began to love literacy and requested that our tutoring sessions go longer and longer each day. He proudly shared his learning with his parents, grandparents, and anyone else who would pause long enough to hear his question, "What is a colloid?" Per completed another reading inventory in August: reading the eighth-grade lists and an expository fifth-grade passage with 100 percent comprehension.

I Love to Read So Much

While I'd seen the change in Per's attitude, engagement, and motivation around literacy, I didn't expect six grade levels of progress in isolated words and a four-grade-level jump in reading comprehension. As we were talking about these accomplishments, this eight-year-old interrupted to say, "There really *is* nothing I can't read. That's why I like doing it now. That little boy has wanted to read since he was six." I knew that Per was poised for success in third grade and in life. Per has since told his father, "I might be a librarian when I grow up because I love to read so much."

All things were possible when I stopped being a teacher on a time line and became a mirror of Per's needs and desires by turning them into immediate, engaging, and relevant literacy experiences. No more stomachache—instead, a real mission accomplished.

A Special Boy Teaches
Us Special Lessons

William P. Bintz and Pamela L. Wright

*Children's responses are nearly always
worth the wait.*

—KEENE AND ZIMMERMANN, 2007; P. 152

LIKE MANY TEACHERS, WE'RE GETTING PRETTY GOOD at waiting.
We've been waiting for the public to regard all teachers as professionals, communities to pass needed school levies, districts
to increase teacher salaries, supervisors to purchase new curriculum resources, coordinators to provide more meaningful
professional development opportunities, and parents to recognize and appreciate the artistry needed to teach their children effectively. We're still waiting and still hopeful. We're just
not sure if it's really worth the wait. What we are sure of is this:
waiting for children's responses is worth the wait. Here's one
example.

Today was special because it was filled with unexpected sur-
prises from a little boy that resulted in *Aha!* moments for his
teachers. "Annie Blevins" had invited us into her second-grade

classroom to conduct a demonstration lesson on reading and writing. Today, something special happened.

We shared two award-winning wordless picture books: *The Red Book* (Lehman, 2004) and *One Scary Night* (Guillopp, 2005). Each is an engaging text and promotes the notion of reading as meaning making, which, according to Annie, is a view of reading her students need to experience. Each is an example of thoughtful text—texts that include layers of meanings, invite multiple interpretations, and require readers to deal with anomalies and ambiguities to make sense of the story. Each enables children to create words for the text and supports written response to text.

We noticed that one student . . . was struggling to get anything down on paper. He was writing letters and words, but no sentences.

We told the students that we wanted to share two books. Each had no words because somebody took them. We didn't know who took the words or where they took them. We just knew that the words were gone and we needed to put them back. The students were ready to help.

First, we did a picture walk through *The Red Book*. Afterward, students gave oral retellings of what the story meant to them. We used "what the story means to you" as a prompt because we wanted students to share personal meanings of the story. We celebrated different interpretations. Next, we read aloud *One Scary Night*. We invited students to "give this book back its words" by writing a sentence or two on Post-it notes for each page and sharing their writing with the entire class. We also stopped approximately two-thirds of the way through the story and asked students to make a prediction about what was going to happen next. The chosen page represents a pivotal point in the story. The next page reveals the surprising ending. We asked students to reflect on the story so far and write a retelling based on their current understanding. We also invited them to predict and write in the retelling how they thought the story would end. They went right to work.

We noticed that one student, "Ben," was struggling to get anything down on paper. He was writing letters and words, but no sentences. Afterward, we invited students to share their writing. Students described how the story is about a wolf following a boy in the woods during a snowstorm, waiting to pounce on him and eat him. In actual fact, this is what the author wants readers to believe at this point in the story. He wants to give readers the impression that the animal is a wolf, or as one student said, "the wolf is a predator." The next page, however, reveals the true story. Ben didn't need the next page.

Ben raised his hand immediately and excitedly volunteered to share his understanding of the story. We were surprised because Ben still had not written much on his paper. We were curious then, and a little bit apprehensive, about what he was about to share. He said: "It's not about a wolf trying to eat the boy. It's about a dog that's trying to save the boy." There was a collective "What?" voiced by other students. He continued: "Go back a page. See the animal jumping at the boy? It looks like he is attacking him. That's what I first thought. But then I saw the tree. See, the tree is leaning and about to fall. Now, turn the page. See? The tree has fallen. And it would have fallen right on top of the boy, but the dog leaped on him, not to eat him, but to save him by getting him out of the way of the falling tree." There was a collective "Cool!" and "Oh, wow!" and "I didn't see that!"

Ben was proud of himself and we were proud of him. Later, Annie and the two of us talked about the lesson. Annie started.

She had a big smile on her face. In fact, she almost had tears in her eyes. She said: "You don't know this, but Ben is a special education student who doesn't participate in many class activities, no matter what I try. When he does participate, he isn't very successful. He struggles with written language. That's why I wasn't surprised about his lack of writing today. What I was so surprised about was that he was the only child today who saw the tree falling and put that and other clues together to make a great inference. Quite frankly, I didn't see the tree leaning and certainly didn't infer that it was falling. That was great. I've never seen him more engaged, more excited about sharing, and more thoughtful about his reading. I couldn't be more proud of him."

We all agreed that Ben was special child—not because he was in special education, but because he taught us some special lessons. Here are a few:

- When students are struggling with literacy, like Ben, change the nature of the curriculum, not the nature of the learner.
- Never underestimate the power and potential of engaging literature, particularly with struggling readers.
- Text selection and social engagement are critical to teach reading comprehension and inferential thinking.
- Remember that some children think well, even though they may not read well.
- Children's responses, as Ben's shows, are always worth the wait.

Thank you, Ben. Because of you, we are better teachers. You have really been worth the wait.

Authors' Note: The two of us conduct collaborative, classroom-based action research in Paducah schools as part of an innovative professional development program across the district. This program focuses on using high-quality and award-winning literature as tools to teach across the curriculum.

Kids Become Better Readers . . . by Reading!

Kathy A. Egawa

Aaron's mother didn't know what to make of these results—as a fourth grader Aaron could readily name colors and objects, for instance—but when I offered to work with him, she hurriedly added that he read like a kindergartner.

I SENSED A SUBTLE SHIFT IN HER VOICE as my physician's assistant, "Kathy Franklin," talked about her sons. They were amazing kids and skilled athletes, yet the younger son, "Aaron," was unhappy and struggling to learn. The independent school he attended requested that he get professional tutoring, as they were not able to teach him.

Recent testing the parents had arranged at the school's request—the fifth such major battery of tests Aaron had faced—had resulted in a diagnosis of "language-based learning disability, symptomatic of an underlying language processing disorder and dyslexic-like delays in reading and writing; attention regulation challenges."

Aaron's scores on two hours of testing began with 82 percent on the Peabody Picture Vocabulary Test and plummeted to less than the pre-primer level on the Woodcock Johnson, 8 percent on auditory discrimination and sequential recall of phonological information, and below the first percentile on "rapid naming of colors in rows and of drawn objects."

Kathy didn't know what to make of these results—as a fourth grader Aaron could readily name colors and objects, for instance—but when I offered to work with him, she hurriedly added that he read like a kindergartner.

Such authoritative test results and "educational-ese" left the parents apologetic and without a plan of action, even though the reports had been preceded by two years of tutoring, vision testing, and summer school, also prescribed by the school.

His teachers added their own observations:

Aaron is neither recalling nor retaining any information that is being taught, even with reconstructing the information, graphic organizers, oral directions, chunking of information, and one on one explanation. He is still not working at a fourth-grade level of comprehension. A trip to the bathroom takes up most of the silent reading time. He becomes anxious and tries to distract others so they will be less aware of his inability to sit.

Such authoritative test results and "educational-ese" left the parents apologetic and without a plan of action, even though

MOTIVATION

the reports had been preceded by two years of tutoring, vision testing, and summer school, also prescribed by the school. Kathy had followed every new round of advice without success.

I began to work with Aaron two or three times a week, and we continued for the next ten months. In that time he grew two years as a reader. Although clearly a breakthrough, this success has not undone the psychological impact and feelings of difference created by his earlier experiences.

Here is a summary of the plan of action and structure that I used with Aaron:

Get to Know the Learner

I learned a lot about Aaron at our first meeting. He loves sports and his dog. His father is a chef and photographer and Aaron shares these interests.

I took along several short texts so that I could assess Aaron's strengths and miscues while reading. The first was too difficult, and Aaron sped through it skipping 40 percent of the text, reading so quietly that I couldn't accurately follow along. He was more successful on a simpler text, but again read quickly at a whisper. He answered, "I don't know" to most of the questions on the Burke Reading Interview. I knew I needed to regroup and observe him in successful learning experiences. This could be a challenge with a kid who reported that he had never read a book.

I began our next meeting with a playful picture book about a dog. We read side by side and Aaron chimed in with some of the reading. We then located several books on soccer, browsed them, and I noted his close scrutiny of the illustrations. I also took along several simpler, more predictable texts and read several to him, and then with him.

Create a Learning Structure

Over the next month, my work with Aaron evolved into an instructional structure for our reading time together and for family members who also worked with him.

1. *Shared Reading* (30–45 minutes): I introduced a series of "just right" books, read through each once, and then shared the reading with Aaron. After two readings, these became part of the familiar book collection.
2. *Independent Reading* (20–30 minutes): Aaron read aloud from the familiar book collection, marking each reading on a chart. Several became favorites and over several months he read them more than ten times each.
3. *Read Aloud* (20–30 minutes): I read short chapter books aloud, with Aaron reading parts for various characters. Favorites included *The Enormous Crocodile* (Dahl) and *Stone Fox* (Gardiner).
4. *Explorers Club* (30–45 minutes): We used reading and writing to study a topic of keen interest—crows. We observed and photographed crows, read books, and produced a multimedia report.

Most important, I asked Kathy not to interrupt or to help Aaron if he got stuck or made mistakes when reading. Slowly he began to trust and use the strategies we discussed, some of which I think he had developed over years of his mother's nightly bedtime reading with him.

One favorite moment caught on video is Aaron counting the books he had read in twenty minutes: "See how many books I read? *Gorillas at the Zoo, The Smallest Mouse, The Wise Old Owl, The Birthday Surprise, The Night Visitor, The Trophy, The Magic Show,* and *The Field Trip.* That's eight books! One, two, three, four, five, six, seven, eight!" (These books are recommended in DeFord, 2004.) Kids become better readers . . . by reading!

Educators Can Take Their Lead from Children

A commitment to teaching as inquiry is a commitment to assess, teach, revise, assess, and teach again. There is more to Aaron's story than I can share here, but his experience is a reminder that, in the end, educators can take their lead from children or from programs and tests. The lenses and tools we use affect what we see. Early in my career, my focus was on the required programs and tests; then a child interrupted that limited view. Since that time, taking an inquiry stance—that is, asking what a learner knows and can do and if my teaching supports new learning—is the stance that best serves my work.

The Mattie Club: Created by Children Who Love Poetry and Life

Lindsay P. Grow

We stand unafraid to express ourselves,
but to show our inside out through
the eyes of poetry.

IT WAS ONE OF THE FEW "THROW THE LESSON PLAN entirely out the window" experiences I've encountered. The fifth-grade writing lesson was supposed to be about using the five senses to create images for the reader. As a model we were discussing poems written by Mattie Stepanek (2002), a young poet who died at the age of fourteen from a rare form of muscular dystrophy.

But the kids took that lesson somewhere entirely different. They didn't want to just talk about how Mattie used senses to get the images across; they wanted to dig deeper. Deeper into the reasons Mattie wrote the poems, the themes and lessons of his poems, his inspirations.

They questioned each other and said things like, "I'm making an inference that Mattie means he wishes he didn't have so much pain, but that he's happy anyway."

Another child responded, "I wonder why he has so much hope?"

"I'm impressed with how much of a difference he made."

"Yeah, how old was he? And he published a book!"

Their faces lit up, so many hands were wiggling in the air; the excitement was hard to contain. These children were feeling inspired, inspired to make a difference, to dig deep within themselves to see what they could do to change the world. Sometimes motivating children who are at and above grade level to work to their potential is challenging; this was a situation where motivation was not a problem.

Looking around me, I could see this lesson was going to be about more than the five senses. I took a deep breath and put my lesson plans aside, saying, "Go back to your seats. I'm going to play some soft music, and I want you to write about some of the things that are deep in your hearts."

Looking around me, I could see this lesson was going to be about more than the five senses. I took a deep breath and put my lesson plans aside, saying, "Go back to your seats. I'm going to play some soft music, and I want you to write about some of the things that are deep in your hearts." I gave them a few more instructions, to make sure all the children felt they would have something to write about, and then I set them loose.

As I circulated, I was in awe of some of the writing. The paraprofessional whispered anxiously to me several times when she spotted kids writing in ways they never had before. Silently, tears streamed down one child's face; as I whispered with that child, I discovered she was unlocking some deep fears from her heart in her writing.

Before long, several volunteers wanted to share their compositions with the class. The poetry was sensational; experimental in form, but the content from the majority of pieces showed a new level of depth. One child, Christina Trigoutis (age ten), wrote:

Life is about hope and hope
is about believing in yourself
instead of focusing on all the mistakes
you've made or all the things
you can't do, think about
the good things in life
like your family and
the people you love
around you, at
least that's
what I want
my life to be.

So that day began the Mattie Club. I invited kids to come eat lunch with me to continue working on their poems. Unprompted by me, they came up with the name and a mission:

We stand unafraid
to express ourselves
but to show our
inside out
through the eyes of poetry.

I just provided a place, once a week, to eat lunch and learn about poems. They gave each other assignments to learn about different poets and try out interesting styles of poetry. The club adopted a bulletin board in the room where they could display their writing and poems they enjoyed. Each member had a journal for experimentation with the joy of words.

We celebrated at the culmination of our formal poetry unit with a Poetry Café. Gourmet desserts, special cookies, "real coffee," and even café lattes sat atop hand-decorated tablecloths in the media center. Students in the Mattie Club organized the event and each had a role to make the celebration a success: greeters, servers, decorators, master of ceremonies. The whole class participated, using a microphone to share a poem from their anthology, and displaying their accompanying artwork using a document camera.

Powerfully Connect with a Few Students

The Mattie Club was something we looked forward to; it was a place I was able to powerfully connect with a few students, a place to challenge them and to affirm them. Finding a way to plan something big that the students helped organize was motivating. Giving them jobs and making them responsible made them part of the team.

Take advantage of your students' interests, and let your interests be contagious. I love poetry and let it really show to my students on the day I threw my lesson plan out the window. Kids pick up on passion.

Embracing moments of student interest and finding ways to be learner centered is essential. Finding ways to connect with students, to show them they are valued and to support their interests, brings rewards for the student and invigorates the teacher.

My Opinion: No One Ever Asked Before

Lisa Janes

In the next few weeks, I noticed a huge change in Eddie's attitude and behavior. He was interested in reading and didn't mind writing.

FOR THE PAST SEVERAL YEARS, I have tried to figure out how to get my boy students engaged in reading and writing. Well, I think I finally got it. Last year, I was teaching fifth grade when one of my boys brought in this book his father bought him. It was titled *The Day My Butt Went Psycho.* As he showed it to me, I thought to myself, "Are you kidding me? His father bought him this book, and let him bring it to school." However, what I actually said was, "Wow, Chris, that is an interesting book. Please let me know how it is." He went back to his seat, and I hoped the book would disappear. What I observed was the complete opposite. The more he read the book, the more curious the boys around him were about reading the book.

Around this time, I had just begun reading journals with my students. They needed to write about the independent books they were reading. Eddie was a student who had transferred in and really had no desire to read. While he was a great reader, he would not pick up a book unless he was forced to read. To my surprise, Eddie turned in his reading journal early that week. However, to my dismay as I began reading his journal, I realized that Chris had lent his book to Eddie. My first thought was "I am in so much trouble. My student is writing about flying butts attacking." Yet as I read on I realized Eddie wrote me an awesome journal entry. He began with "Dear Mrs. Janes, I am reading *The Day My Butt Went Psycho.*" He went on to describe what a ridiculous crazy book it was, and how much he enjoyed reading it. He had turned in a two-page entry to me describing in detail all about the flying butts and the attacks in the story. Then, I realized, *wait a minute, he is reading and writing!* This was my goal, and he now has a book he couldn't put down. What an amazing moment. However, the part that made me speechless was when I came to the sentence that stated his opinion. He said, "I never shared my opinion with anybody else. No one ever asked me my opinion before!" He also made sure to tell me to write back as soon as I could.

My moral would be, find your boys' interest to help them find a book to read, or simply get the most disgusting book you can find and introduce it.

It Took One Book to Reach Out

In the next few weeks, I noticed a huge change in Eddie's attitude and behavior. He was interested in reading and didn't mind writing. I can't believe it took a father to buy a book for his son and the son to share the book with eventually my whole class to get these fifth-grade boys interested in reading. By the end of the school year, more than half of my students had read the book and the two other novels in the series. There was a waiting list for the books! I wanted to share this story because I cannot believe it took one book to reach out and open up so much learning.

My moral would be, find your boys' interest to help them find a book to read, or simply get the most disgusting book you can find and introduce it. Let them write about it. Pretend you hate it or love it! It does not matter, as long as you ask them their opinion! They will share opinions if you ask!

Spiderman to the Rescue

Daniel T. Holm

*Sam was now in his element. He took off with
this project at a run and never looked back.
He spent any extra class time working on his comic,
as well as hours at home. He carefully selected
the words to be used to convey the feelings of
his characters, and he used colored pencils to
provide rich details in each comic frame. Sam,
my reluctant reader and writer, was anything
but a reluctant reader and writer.*

I DISCOVERED THE JOYS OF READING WHEN I was in the sixth grade.
During that year, I had a teacher who knew I could read, knew I
could learn to read better, and knew that I needed interesting
things to read. This teacher, Mr. Holbreck, had a profound impact on my life by guiding me to a path of seeing reading as a
journey of discovery.

My experience of moving from being a reluctant reader to an
avid reader grew over time. I read books about Native Americans

after exploring Pacific coast middens with Mr. Holbreck. I read the directions in order to build Revel race car and Rat Fink models. I became lost in the adventures of Superboy, Brainiac, and Saturn Girl and other members of the Legion of Super-heroes as I read *Adventure* comics. I was a typical boy reader. Now, as an adult with thirty years well spent as an educator, I have learned many lessons about the unique needs readers bring into the classroom. And although I have learned many lessons, working with many students over the years, the story that I tell here deals with my experience with "Sam," a sixth-grade student, or using the British term, a grade six student, in London, England.

Sam was now in his element. He took off with this project at a run and never looked back. He spent any extra class time working on his comic, as well as hours at home.

After teaching at Indiana University South Bend for six years, I was missing the opportunity of working with elementary-age students. I applied and was approved for a one-year sabbatical. My sabbatical project involved returning to an elementary school classroom. My options: teach in Indiana or teach in England. After about three seconds of deliberation, I chose England. Once all of the work visa materials were finalized, I found myself during the 2001–2002 school year teaching grade six in London.

I went to my teaching assignment with fifteen years of class-room experience and six years of university teaching experience. I was excited, scared, and looking forward to trying some new instructional strategies with my students. After becoming acclimated to my new teaching situation and understanding the British curriculum, I was ready to greet my twenty-eight grade six students.

I brought with me many books and materials from the United States to share with my students. I figured that many of the students would want to know what sixth-grade students in the United States were interested in. I was right. My grade six students were fascinated with the books, sports, pop culture, and even pencils that American students are exposed to. (Note: British students do not have number two pencils; their pencils are a little fatter and have separate erasers, which in England are called rubbers.)

Sharing about America and learning about my students turned into an ongoing process. I learned that "Jason" was interested in writing and performing rap. I learned that "Catherine" was interested in architecture. And I learned "Majabeen" enjoyed writing. I also learned that "Sam," although a very good reader, did not find reading exciting. He simply wanted to draw comic characters.

It was easy to find ways to encourage interests in rap, and architecture, and writing. But what could I do to promote comic drawing, and how would promoting comic drawing engage Sam in reading and writing?

After some reflection, I decided that I would introduce the class to superheroes. I decided on a class exploration of super-heroes, and of course their necessary counterparts, supervillians. I knew a fair amount about the topic from my childhood days, and, in fact had brought materials to England in anticipation of conducting a unit on superheroes. Sam's reluctance as a reader and writer helped to drive the project. I wanted to help Sam become excited about reading and writing. So, I introduced Sam and the class to superheroes through comic books.

Many of the students were unfamiliar with various superhero characters, so I introduced the students to Superman, who was my own childhood hero. We charted out his characteristics on a large chart board, which would later be used for other characters. We found out about how he became super, his life growing up, his friends, his powers or abilities, his secret identity, his weaknesses, and his enemies.

I then broke the students into research teams. Each team explored, as a group, the characteristics listed on the chart for their group's superhero. In groups of four they used comic books and the Internet to explore Flash, Green Lantern, Wonder Woman, Batman, Daredevil, Spiderman, and Supergirl. As the groups found information, we completed the large chart we had used for Superman.

After the groups found out information about their characters, we had a class sharing time to look at similarities and differences across the characters. This initial research and sharing took a week, with about one hour to an hour and a half each day. Throughout this process I observed Sam being actively engaged and going beyond class time and resources to find out more about Spiderman (his group's character). This pleased me, as it is what I hoped would happen.

Once we compared and contrasted the characters, it was time to move to the next stage of developing a superhero or supervillian on their own. I provided the students with a graphic organizer patterned after the chart on the board: powers, friends, secret identity, and so on. The students each individually or in pairs completed the chart as part of their prewriting. It should be noted here that although this graphic organizer was part of their prewriting, they had in fact been prewriting all along as they researched the characteristics of superheroes in their groups.

Once I approved their graphic organizers, the students in their partner pairs or on their own proceeded to create a superhero or supervillain comic book. To assist them with this process, we again turned back to the comic books that I had available to analyze how the writer and illustrator presented the stories.

Sam was now in his element. He took off with this project at a run and never looked back. He spent any extra class time working on his comic, as well as hours at home. He carefully selected the words to be used to convey the feelings of his characters, and he used colored pencils to provide rich details in each comic frame. Sam, my reluctant reader and writer, was anything but a reluctant reader and writer. In fact, once the students saw Sam's illustrations and text, many wanted him to be their partner.

Move to the Path of Wanting to Read and Write

The development of the comics took over two weeks. Once the books were completed, the students shared their work with the rest of the class. This project was a success. The students were excited throughout the process. I was especially pleased with Sam's responses, since he was the one student I was primarily trying to move to the path of wanting to read and write. It worked. He continued to read and write using comic characters throughout the year. And in time, I was able to get him interested in reading graphic novels, which were a logical next step in getting him excited about reading.

My work with Sam reinforced for me two important lessons. The first: share what you know, because what is exciting to you as the teacher can excite students. I did this for Sam and the rest of the class, by exposing them to a childhood interest of mine. The second: many materials can lead a person to the joys of reading. Even though as teachers and parents we want learners to read books, sometimes we need to get students excited with non-book reading as a way to get them started on the journey of reading.

Graphic novels are finding their way into schools and are becoming very popular with children as a genre of choice when asked to select a book to read. What is important when using comic books or graphic novels as teaching tools is to teach children about text features. In most cases, students need to learn how to read the bubble thoughts, and this type of reading requires a different way of teaching. Consider taking a trip to the library and have your librarian show your class the different types of comic books and graphic novels that are now available. Pick out a few of your favorites in advance and read them to the children upon your return.

Reflections on the Breakthroughs

Susan E. Israel

WHAT I ENJOYED MOST ABOUT THE STORIES in this part was the natural realization that book selection processes are important to creating a mutual respect between the child and the adult. Personalizing book selections goes beyond simply providing students with choices. The power of the stories and types of literature makes a difference in learning outcomes. New genres and unusual books such as wordless picture books and humorous books as well as alternative methods such as oral reading can all enhance motivation and play a significant role in achieving literacy breakthroughs.

One lesson I learned from Part Two is that teachers need to allow students to enjoy books they regard as theirs. I can recall several experiences with my own children when they came home and told me about a book their teacher would not let them read during independent reading time. Was I to challenge the teacher and insist that she let my daughter read a book about how to use the Internet, or tell my daughter to select another book? Respect is demonstrated when children are valued enough to allow opportunities to communicate what they value. Use the questions in this summary to help you reflect on the importance of books and selection of books being used to teach reading and writing.

Breakthrough Elements

The stories in this part offer ideas about providing opportunities for children to make choices related to what they want to read or write about.

Although the element of book choice is present in the stories, the concept goes beyond providing an abundance of selections, variety, or options based on the child's interests. We need to consider how choices offered to the student will best support literacy growth. The stories invite us to think more deeply about what it means to personalize literature selections for students in order to develop their literacy skills. In the story by Danna Parsons, we learn that by choosing a short and humorous chapter book she was able to capture the attention and mind of one of her most restless students and set him on the path to literacy learning. The piece by Emily Manning helps us understand that stories with powerful messages, such as *The Lorax,* can have a profound impact on students, even requiring the teacher to depart from the lesson plan. In this case, the lesson resulted in a student-generated tree-planting project to make the world a better place. Elizabeth Frye shows that wordless picture books can be powerful tools for inspiring young reluctant writers who have difficulty imagining and crafting stories. She helped her students realize success by providing them with a safe collaborative environment where they could view themselves as authors. Karen Jorgensen's story describes how Dav Pilkey's *Captain Underpants,* a humorous tale with cartoon-like drawings, helped transform Per, a struggling learner of English, into a confident reader. Her book choices related to the child's own interests were important, but she also asked a key question: "What is the minimum that needs to happen to get Per to change his attitude about reading?"

In the piece by William Bintz and Pamela Wright, we learn not only how a particular story inspired Ben, a special needs student, to participate in class discussion, but how his unique interpretation led the entire class to a literacy breakthrough. Kathy Egawa describes how she enabled Aaron, a young student with reading disabilities, to overcome his learning barriers and succeed at reading by introducing him to books that connected with his personal interests, in this case dogs and sports. Impressed by how her fifth-grade class responded to the poetry of Mattie Stepanek, Lindsay Grow describes how she found it important to help her students establish a club to build on their literary interests and explore their own creative world in writing. Lisa Janes and Daniel Holm in their respective stories talk about use of unusual literature to motivate and instruct their students. Janes discovers that *The Day My Butt Went Psycho,* a book that some teachers might find inappropriate, was especially appealing to the boys in her class, and this warmed her to the idea of using humor genres for literacy instruction. Holm, in turn, describes how showing his personal passion for comic book heroes made a breakthrough that was life changing for his students, especially boys.

The authors' stories leave us to contemplate some different or difficult questions. Is the text choice available the best one for the student relative to the task? Will the alternative options I provide result in literacy goal attainment? Will the text result in increased levels of learning? Who makes the final choice when choices are an option? Personalizing books is more than just allowing students to select books of their choosing whenever they want. It is about selecting and teaching from books that are personalized for the student, small group, or class that are also appropriate for the instructional task or goal.

Aside from choice, what I find notable in these stories is that teachers working with the most at-risk students do not settle for lower standards. Instead, they encourage students to read harder books of interest rather than easy-readers they can read but find boring. The stories were selected for this section because they each featured a particular book that had an impact on students' learning. Directly or indirectly, the teachers showed us that because of the text something else was discovered.

- When selecting books for students, does the reading level of the text matter?
- How can other genres be used effectively to help children learn to read?
- Why do most parents and teachers ignore valuable print-rich material like comic books or magazines?
- How can I help the student I am concerned about learn to love books as much as I do?
- What books or topics do I know a lot about that I can share with my students to motivate them to learn more?
- What can I learn from this book that might help me understand how technology will impact reading and writing?
- Do you think understanding your own habits of book selections can also help you be a better teacher and professor of literacy?
- Do the classroom resources available in your teaching environment meet the needs of the children who you are most concerned about?

Lessons Learned

The stories in this part teach three primary lessons about reading and writing. Choice is important, but it needs to be made in correlation with overall goals of the child and the curriculum. Teachers need to be able to explain why they are choosing to do this rather than that. Purposeful choices are more valuable than random ones. Second, allow children to use literature as a means to create and develop broader student-generated goals that make the world a better place. Teachers in this part allowed children time to plant trees, start clubs, read and write poetry and comics. The literature expanded the mind and the heart in ways that helped the children make literacy breakthroughs. Last, teachers need to ask metacognitive questions about their literature choices: Why am I reading this to my children? Why did I allow my students to read this book? What is the minimum I need to be doing to help this child overcome reading fears? The teachers in Part Two used their stories to help us hear their thinking that went on when they were making decisions. This will help you understand that genres can empower and motivate reluctant readers and writers. Sharing your own talents and personal interests helps students expand literary horizons in a meaningful and motivational manner. Instill a value in children that resource selections do make a difference and don't give up until you find that one text that reaches out and opens a child's mind and heart. When teacher reflection leads to change, the door for student reflection opens, and change occurs. Both teacher and student learn personal lessons.

Ten Literacy Breakthrough Actions You Can Take Today

1. Right now make a list of the books you are using with the students you are trying to help. Ask yourself, Why is this book important to use?
2. If you are teaching a specific strategy related to reading, are you using books that will support that strategy? Are there better materials you can use?

3. Do you have a favorite genre or book series that you can share with your class? Bring that book or collection to show the students during the next read-aloud and tell them why these books were important to you. Do not expect them to be interested in these books; instead, ask them what books they are interested in.
4. If you are working with a reluctant speaker in your classroom, pair this child with a more capable peer when asked to read aloud in class.
5. Bring in a graphic novel appropriate for your age group and teach the students how to read this type of book.
6. Write a class book of funny stories and make a copy for everyone in your class.
7. Consider labeling space on your bookshelf for each child in your class. Invite the children to make tags that read, "[Myname]'s Books."
8. Ask your students what books they prefer to read.
9. Bring in funny stories to read to the students during read-aloud time.
10. Make a list of books that you notice your students reading. Use this list to share new book ideas with your students. For example, say "If you like to read . . . you might also like to read books like this. . . . " Share more titles with them. You might even take time to type the book titles into Amazon.com and check out other books students are reading on the same topic.

Further Reading

When you need to get students thinking differently: *The Three Questions* by Jon J. Muth (New York: Scholastic, 2002). The text in this book is something every child can relate to, that is, asking questions. The main character is a boy who is trying to find the answers to three inspirational questions. Use this book to demonstrate to students how to ask questions that are also insightful and that go beyond what is obvious. This will begin the development of ideas on any topic you are working on.

When you want to help students understand that reading is something that should be enjoyable: Children's literature is a wonderful tool to enhance literacy instruction and to motivate children to read. *Using Children's Literature in Preschool: Comprehending and Enjoying Books* by Leslie Mandel Morrow and Linda B. Gambrell (Newark, Del.: International Reading Association, 2004) is a rich resource with ideas on children's literature that can be integrated into all aspects of the preschool curriculum.

When you want to think differently about your book selections: My own *Dynamic Literacy Instruction* (Norwood, Mass.: Christopher-Gordon, 2008) discusses goal setting and literacy instruction based on standards and teaching dispositions. Key elements in the book focus on understanding the needs of our students. Creative lessons and further recommendations on how teachers can evaluate their disposition as a teacher are included in each section.

When you want a resource that moves from theory to practice on learning words: *Bringing Words to Life: Robust Vocabulary Instruction* by Isabel L. Beck, Margaret G. McKeown, and Linda Kucan (New York: Guilford Press, 2002) is a quick read that teaches integrated vocabulary strategies with children's literature and print-rich material. The authors also provide tiered lessons for students at different ability levels.

When you are looking for books specifically for boys: John Scieska's Web site (www.guysread.com) includes book recommendations specifically for boys. What is unique about this site is that it is managed by a famous children's author who shares his early reading experiences. Teachers can use this site to find specific books and topics of interest to boys while at the same time promoting literacy through reading and writing.

When you are looking for books specifically for girls: A great resource to learn about what girls like to read can be found by searching Amazon.com or any general bookstore Web site. You can type in keywords such as Girls and Reading, What Girls Are Reading, or Books for Girls. Next you can narrow your focus by age group or topic. In most cases, I have found that girls like to read series books, self-help books, books on friendships, communication, and getting along with parents. Girls also like to read lots of fairy-tale and fantasy books because they like to imagine and pretend. I have found this to be the best search approach because it focuses on personalizing the literature selections based on what you are specifically looking for. If I do this and still cannot find what I am looking for, I usually go to the library and ask the resource librarian, "What books are being checked out the most by this age group?"

Engagement

MULTISENSORY
EXPERIENCES

About the Stories

Susan E. Israel

WHY DO YOU REMEMBER WHEN YOU were growing up and getting your first box of crayons? What I know about children is they love to be engaged in activities, games, or anything that is interactive and hands-on. Kids love to be entertained, but they also love the idea of creating things. My own children always wanted me to buy them new crayons or markers. They loved blank sheets of paper or spiral-bound drawing books. There is something very special about being involved with activities that inspire creativity while at the same time inviting learning to take place.

Part Three contains stories that will inspire readers to motivate students to learn by engaging them in multisensory experiences. *Multisensory* is a term used to explain the multiple ways to approach learning using sensory stimulus as the primary instructional platform. These types of teaching techniques introduce learning from an oral, visual, tactile, or kinesthetic perspective and engage the child in instructional activities involving varied senses. For example, from an oral perspective, teachers might use verbal illustrations or stories to communicate and teach.

Multisensory approaches to learning make learning engaging while at the same time fostering increased reading and writing development. As in the stories in Part Two, teachers incorporate personalized multisensory approaches either discovered naturally by the teacher or provided by the student through observations, demonstrations, or evaluations.

The stories in this part focus on unusual learners, including children who are less verbal, who live in different perceptual worlds, or who might be considered at-risk in reading, writing, or developmentally. Terry Atkinson uses a variety of hands-on play activities to work with a child with unusual gifts. Nina Nilsson links visual instructional methods with tactile activities to give attention to the child's unusual perceptual abilities. Amelia Evans and Mariana Souto-Manning integrate the use of oral, visual, and tactile methods to help toddlers become more engaged in the learning process. Marianne McTavish, with the support of an intergenerational family, makes use of signs and symbols (the visual) to help students understand that print has meaning. Mary Banta, a former reading specialist, helps fifth-grade boys develop their literacy interests by engaging them in a combination of tactile (cutting and laminating comic strips) and visual activities in which the students eventually create their own strips. Sheila Gaquin engages students using all their sensory abilities. She first empowers them through storytelling on tape recorders, but engages all the senses and taps into the child's wisdom of experience. Monique Poldberg closes this section with a wonderful story about how art, which incorporates a variety of senses, can be used as a pathway into literacy.

Learning to Read His Own Way

Terry S. Atkinson

THIS STORY BEGAN DURING THE FIRST YEAR OF MY tenure as a reading specialist in an independent school, when I was invited to work with "Benjamin." Having just heard the diagnosis that their son was learning disabled, Benjamin's parents looked to school administrators and me for advice. A documented discrepancy between scores on ability and achievement tests had clearly identified the reason why their son had failed to learn to read. Enrolling him in a school for students with severe learning difficulties was the recommendation offered by my colleagues.

According to school administrators, Benjamin's kindergarten and first-grade teachers had implemented the school's adopted reading series following publisher's guidelines. By mid-year in first grade, he spent more time in the bathroom when his reading group met than he did in the classroom. As soon as testing was suggested to identify Benjamin's problem, the parents immediately complied.

New in my position as reading specialist, I had spent my first few months researching and designing a resource support for the struggling readers in this K–5 school. Having spent recent years as a public school teacher, I was surprised to find students in this private school who struggled to become readers. School personnel often recommended psychoeducational testing to identify reasons for these students' struggles. This testing phenomenon sent me to bed most nights with more questions than answers ... eventually leading me to enroll in a doctoral program to understand why privileged children mirrored reading behaviors that I had found commonplace among children of poverty.

Although I was a novice at making sense of the psychoeducational testing game, the resulting diagnosis made absolutely no sense to me. How could a precocious first grader be expected to score well on achievement tests if he could not read?

When I was asked by school administrators to attend a meeting with Benjamin's parents, I had not laid eyes on him nor heard him read. Based on the claims of his parents and the testing psychologist that he demonstrated giftedness in many areas, I was dismayed that school officials so readily wrote off this young reader. Although I was a novice at making sense of the psychoeducational testing game, the resulting diagnosis made absolutely no sense to me. How could a precocious first grader be expected to score well on achievement tests if he could not read?

I suggested that Benjamin and I begin working together one-on-one. His parents were particularly enthusiastic about the possibility of individualized help that might help unravel their son's frustration. So this was the genesis of our collaboration ... and Benjamin and I became fast friends.

Meeting daily for whatever time I could borrow from his classroom, I learned that Benjamin had many talents, the most remarkable of which was his ability to craft amazing structures from Lego blocks. When our conversation shifted to books or reading, however, he practically broke out in a sweat. His reading was littered with desperate guessing based on initial consonants, and meaning-making was rare. Strategies that helped other emergent readers did little to derail his failure. Knowing nothing else to do, I looked to him for answers . . . perhaps his strength could save him. Might Legos teach him to read?

And learn he did. He built elaborate Lego buildings and I photographed them in various stages of completion. With each photo glued onto a large page, Benjamin dictated building details that grew in complexity from simple labels to phrases to sentences. As pages became books, we choral read, partner read, and diced and sliced the text in every possible way. Words borrowed from his writing morphed into "games" . . . simple word sorts growing into related word families and sight word decks that he and I competed to read. His books were read at home, to peers, to kindergartners, to anyone who would listen.

Book after book, Benjamin's confidence and competence grew. His collection of personally authored books soon included additional simple nonfiction texts, which he chose based on his interests. Individualized summer support and two years of continued small group intervention led to a reader who could hold his own as he navigated fourth grade.

Build on the Familiar

Literacy professor Linda Gambrell (Gambrell, 1996) states that making a real difference in the literacy lives of children is "not an exact science." The important lesson to learn in this story is that not all reading methodologies fit every student. Unlocking the door to reading for Benjamin and others who struggle requires looking beyond publishers' one-size-fits-all methods. In this particular case, learning to read his own way allowed Benjamin to build on the familiar and have a huge hand in unlocking the door for himself.

If They Can't Learn the Way We Teach, Maybe We Should Teach the Way They Learn

Nina L. Nilsson

My mother's name also was Elizabeth. And, similarly, my mother had experienced difficulty reading. For her, this disability came toward the end of her life after a series of mini strokes gradually robbed her of her eyesight.

AS A READING SPECIALIST, I always listen to what parents have to say before beginning my work with struggling readers. Intuitively, they know when their children's progress is not on track. Yet the exact nature of their children's reading difficulties often eludes them. "No one," this mother said in explaining her reason for contacting me, "has been able to teach Elizabeth to read."

Born two months premature, Elizabeth was no stranger to the hospital. At one point, she was diagnosed with mild cerebral palsy. After a neurological evaluation, however, the signs were inconclusive. Various assessments of motor skills, cognitive functioning, and communicative development concurred; Elizabeth's progress in all these areas fell outside the normal range. In general, Elizabeth achieved developmental milestones later than expected.

When Elizabeth showed up for our first session a week later, I was struck by how small she appeared for her ten years of age. As always, I began with assessments. However, only with time did I grow to learn her glaring weaknesses and her savant-like strengths. During this first session, I learned which letters and numerals she recognized. I also discovered the only word she could read: "Elizabeth."

When she began the task of reading the print, her knowledge of the story line helped her negotiate the words. It even let her read whole sentences that were complex and that, out of context, would overwhelm her linguistic abilities.

My mother's name also was Elizabeth. And, similarly, my mother had experienced difficulty reading. For her, this disability came toward the end of her life after a series of mini strokes gradually robbed her of her eyesight. During this first session, I took Elizabeth by the hand and led her into my kitchen. "I want to show you something special to me. Look." Standing before a wall covered with framed pictures, I pointed to a crude yellow and black needlepoint. This was a piece of artwork my mother created in 1929 when she, also, was just ten years of age. Stitched onto the canvas is a large yellow rectangle house topped with a smaller yellow rectangle chimney, with black stitches forming the background and green lettering which spells out her name. With fixed gaze, she paused. "Elizabeth," she read with sudden recognition. A smile radiated across her face.

What began as two hours a week expanded into six, for soon I realized that to make any kind of difference in Elizabeth's reading ability, I needed more time. And when her private day school no longer seemed to meet Elizabeth's needs, Barbara found Karen, another parent at the school who was also searching for a more personalized education for her daughter. Karen offered to home-school Elizabeth along with her own daughter, a few years younger than Elizabeth. So Elizabeth went to Karen's for her "school day," then she came to me three afternoons a week for reading instruction. When Karen dropped off Elizabeth, we frequently shared our utter amazement at some unusual talent Elizabeth had displayed—a sudden emerging skill that we'd noted, a new clue into the way Elizabeth's mind worked.

"B," Elizabeth vocalized as she ran her finger over the sandpaper letter form. She responded to this type of multisensory experience, and so I created many common sight words from textured materials for her to trace. When Elizabeth knew a word cold, we wrote it on an index card and added it to her shoebox "word bank." One day at the end of our session, as we lifted the box, now taped at the corners for reinforcement and awkward to handle with its added weight, the container slipped out of our hands. The file cards scattered across the carpeting. As we picked them up and returned them to her shoebox, Elizabeth and I looked at each other and smiled. It was at that moment, I believe, we both realized what a tremendous sight vocabulary she had acquired.

Elizabeth displayed certain idiosyncrasies that fascinated me, partly because they illustrated how differently her perceptual world functioned, but also because they reflected her unique gifts, which I have found in every child with whom I've ever

If They Can't Learn the Way We Teach . . .

worked. Her visual memory astounds everyone who knows her. Within minutes of her arrival, typically, Elizabeth identified all of the changes in my office since her last visit.

After finding all the books added to my collection during the week, as if claiming them as her own, Elizabeth plopped on the couch and firmly set the pile of titles beside her, announcing, "I'm going to look at *all* of these." She looked at me as if asking permission. I smiled, and with total absorption, she slowly flipped through every page of each book, "reading" the stories through the illustrations. At times she commented, noting details I'd overlooked. Without a doubt, her observations of subtleties in the pictures would bring the illustrators pleasure. When she began the task of reading the print, her knowledge of the story line helped her negotiate the words. It even let her read whole sentences that were complex and that, out of context, would overwhelm her linguistic abilities.

Elizabeth exhibited a keen interest in science. I grew to discover my love of animals was equaled or surpassed by Elizabeth's love of birds. Using the clues in the illustrations along with the beginning letters of words, Elizabeth surprised me by reading *pelican* and *toucan* and *sandpiper.*

Although Elizabeth showed increasing growth in literacy skills, her processing of graphic symbols was time-consuming and slow. In the tedium of decoding, meaning often got lost. Together we explored how texts with repetitive structures scaffolded her reading and writing abilities.

Presently teaching at a large university in another state, through e-mail and other means, I am still in touch with "Liz," now twenty-three and working with children in a community day care center. Barbara assures me that Liz maintains her ability to sound out words, enjoys books and magazines, as well as reading greeting cards, food products, billboards, store names, and other sorts of environmental print.

Unconventional Path to Literacy

Despite the barriers, Elizabeth succeeded in learning how to read. As one of her coaches seeking ways to help her along her unconventional path to literacy, I believe my greatest learning can be summed up as follows: "If a child cannot learn the way we teach, maybe we should teach the way they learn" (attributed to Ignacio Estrada).

"I Gotta Touch the Book!" Reading Aloud with Young Toddlers

Amelia C. Evans and Mariana Souto-Manning

*Reading aloud to our children will change
their lives forever.*

—Fox, 2001

IT'S READ-ALOUD TIME IN THE YOUNG TODDLER CLASSROOM. The teacher invites the twelve children to sit down on the floor as she gets ready to read a story. As usual, most of them sit close to the teacher who is about to read the book. As the story starts, one by one, the children scoot closer; soon enough, they are all bunched up, touching each other. They all want to be close to the book, but in the process they get very close to each other. Inevitably, they start bumping into each other and quickly their attention shifts from the book and the story. Soon, comments such as "He hit me!" and "She pushed me!" start being muttered (or yelled). Read-aloud is over shortly after it begins.

This frustrating routine happened at least once a day. Teachers noticed that what was happening was not what was supposed to be happening. They knew how difficult it was for the children to understand the need to stay seated on their bottoms so that the child behind them could see. The students were concerned about whether or not they could see. More than that, they wanted to be close to the book.

Initially, the teachers thought that maybe the space was not big enough and that the children did not have enough space. They decided to move outside for read-aloud. Maybe having read-aloud after playing in the playground would solve the issue. The children would have used some of their energy playing and would be ready to sit down and pay attention. They tried moving the group outside and having read-aloud in the playground. No, it did not work! Issues still persisted as Ms. Amy and the other teachers tried to make read-aloud work.

Initially, the teachers thought that maybe the space was not big enough and that the children did not have enough space. They decided to move outside for read-aloud. Maybe having read-aloud after playing in the playground would solve the issue.

The teachers also gave the children the option of engaging in other activities during read-aloud, emphasizing that read-aloud was optional. While that helped, it mostly let children with these issues walk away and not experience read-aloud. Confronting the issue and trying other solutions was a priority for the teachers.

One day, Ms. Amy brought a pile of books outside and offered to let students choose the book to read. The children could not agree at first. They each wanted to read their favorite story. Amy told them that they could read the books individually after read-aloud. So, at the end of read-aloud, they would have a chance to read their book of choice.

This simple action allowed the children to sit through the read-aloud without wanting to get close to the book being read. They knew they would get a turn at reading, touching a book and turning the pages. They were especially interested in reading and touching the big books often used for read-alouds. As they read independently, they practiced reading aloud themselves. Despite the fact that there were multiple copies of some of the most popular books, when two of them were interested in the same book, they often read aloud to each other—not taking turns, but reading concurrently. They checked with each other for understanding as they read the pictures or relied on their memories to retell the stories. For example, some of the patterns in the books would be repeated verbatim. Slowly, this simple solution drew more children to participate in read-aloud and solved some of the behavioral issues that threatened (and many times stopped) the activity.

After read-aloud, children would choose their book and have the opportunity to read it themselves. They sat down and paged through the books, told stories, and started recognizing the books by their titles.

Many emergent literacy skills were fostered in this setting. Surely some pages were torn as children turned pages and eventually some of the books had to be replaced. Nevertheless, in engaging with books, they were acquiring important skills and could participate in the read-alouds without stepping on each other's toes.

"I Gotta Touch the Book!"

"What Does This Say?" A Small Request with Huge Implications

Marianne McTavish

Teaching is the achievement of shared meaning.

—D. B. GOWIN

OUR INTERGENERATIONAL FAMILY LITERACY PROGRAM was a novel project. We were working with a small group of low-literate Sudanese refugee mothers, basing our literacy instruction on building skills and strategies while the mothers learned to read and write the different texts that were central to their lives. As the early childhood literacy instructor, I was working with the preschoolers of these mothers, providing the children with authentic experiences with print in their world and involving them in experiences with reading and writing texts that they recognized as part of their world. My lesson objectives were to focus the children on print, emphasize how it worked and how it functioned in the lives of people. My intent of this instructional program was to bring the young students up to the levels of emergent literacy knowledge held by their middle-class peers. I knew that children who lived in homes where the parents read and wrote more often and read and wrote more complex texts began school with higher levels of emergent literacy knowledge. As the parents of the Sudanese children were low-literate in English as well as in their own language, these children did not have an adult who could point out and read print to them or answer their questions about print. The children, who were four and five years old, simply did not have any idea of the purpose or function of print.

I knew that children who lived in homes where the parents read and wrote more often and read and wrote more complex texts began school with higher levels of emergent literacy knowledge.

I had been working with the children on the concept of intentionality—that print carries meaning. To this end, we had spent the past months engaged in authentic activities such as cooking and card making. The children, who had only been in the country a short while, were also adjusting to the new cultural events in which the literacy was embedded. At times it seemed that my teaching was not having any impact on the children, and I felt I was spending most of my time dealing with the social dynamics of this enjoyable but rambunctious group of preschoolers.

One day we had a flood in our classroom, and we had to take the families to an alternate facility. Upon arrival, it soon became apparent that the room was too small to accommodate us all. As it was a beautiful day and the facility was located next to a lovely public park, we decided to go on a "print walk." I was excited by the possibility of finding new texts in this park, perhaps ones the children had not seen before. To this end, I was reading the signs posted around the park to the children, spending particular time at the large sign that told us that we were heading into an environmentally sensitive area and that we needed to be cautious. Heeding this warning, we carefully continued our walk and soon came to a large pond. I became worried as "Nyama" raced ahead, seemingly ready to plunge right in. But she stopped short of a large sign erected near the pond's edge and studied it carefully. Pointing to the print, she yelled to me, "Oh Marianne! What does this say?!!" I stopped and stood still. It was if a light had turned on in Nyama's head. *She knew that print carried meaning.* She knew that the message on the sign needed to be read because it would contain very important information about the pond. Readers of this story may think this insignificant, but for this child, this tiny event and her enormous realization was a true breakthrough. Attainment of this simple concept would serve now as a foundation for Nyama's pathway to literacy.

I read the sign to her and the group, pointing to the words as I read and explaining why the sign was there. From that moment forward, the preschoolers raced around the park, pointing to print and asking me what it said. It was infectious!

Become Curious

This event reminds me once again of the ingredients necessary for working with young children in early childhood literacy programs: activities need to be authentic and purposeful; concepts need to be developed over time and through meaningful contexts; and caring, literate adults need to work side by side with children to answer their questions about their emerging understandings of literacy. These components go far beyond the narrower conception of letter and sound knowledge instruction found in many early childhood literacy programs.

To accomplish this type of instruction, I try to structure the environment and the learning experiences so that students become curious about print in their world. This demands that I must continually "think aloud" with the children so that they can see the purpose behind my use of print. For example, if I forget something, I tell the children that I need to write it down so I will remember it later, and then do it while they watch. As I write on a sticky note, I read my writing out loud as I go along, so that the children see that this writing serves a purpose. Similarly, when we leave the classroom to go somewhere, the children and I write a note to hang on the door to tell people where we have gone and where they can find us. These explicit and purposeful experiences help the children realize that print indeed means something.

Parents can easily accomplish the same activities at home. For example, parents can write their grocery shopping list while thinking aloud. Asking children what they would like from the grocery store and then writing it down while they watch is an excellent way for children to see that print serves a purpose (to remember what to buy). While shopping, parents can point out the print on packages (brand names, ingredients) to their children as they select the correct brand. These simple activities will help children achieve important emergent literacy concepts that will help them once they reach school.

What is important to learn from this story is that concepts need to be developed in meaningful contexts. This usually means through authentic experiences that are meaningful to the child and the situation.

Gifts from My Heart

Mary J. Banta

*Cory, one of the reading students I taught in my
early teaching years, called me a few years ago.
He told me that I had made a difference in his life.
I taught him that he could do it and achieve
great things in life.*

I WAS A YOUNG TEACHER AT THE TIME I met Cory, full of enthusiasm
and on top of the world. I loved teaching students and seeing the
excitement in their faces when they "got it!" I taught remedial
reading to Grades 1 through 5 in a small southern community in
the Midwest. My fifth-grade boys were at a first-grade beginning-
to-read level. They were also some of the most challenging students I had come up against. They had "bad attitude" written all
over them. They would come in late to my classroom and sit
rather sluggishly in their chairs. I tried reading games and a series
of beginning-to-read books about cowboys I thought might interest them. Well, they didn't!

I then got the idea to ask them what their interests were. They told me they liked racing, sports, and comics, so I made some game boards using vocabulary cards. I made a race track and had a horn to get the "horses" out of the starting gate. We used dice, which they loved! I found some toy horses at a local store. I made several other games such as basketball toss and baseball home run. I also found comic books that they liked. We'd read the comics and I'd ask comprehension questions. They even made their own comic books along with characters, plot, and story.

Another idea I used was to collect Sunday comic strips. I'd laminate them (back then, we used Contac paper), cut them into pieces, and number them in sequential order. Students took turns placing the comic strip in order and then reading it out loud to the group.

My fifth-grade boys were at a first-grade beginning-to-read level. They were also some of the most challenging students I had come up against. They had "bad attitude" written all over them.

Actually, I used comic strips with all grade levels. Several comics had no words, which made putting the strip in order somewhat challenging. "Peanuts" and "Henry" were two favorites.

Creative writing students sometimes need a little nudge. One thing I used was Ziploc bags filled with objects: ribbon, rocks, shells, balls, shoelaces, a watch—any small items that could spark interest in creating a story would work. I had a peg board set up with the creative writing prompt bags handy for spurring innovative writing. Students in my remedial classes would read their stories to lower-grade students to help build up their self-esteem. The students would sometimes make puppets and use them to act out their stories.

The activities I have mentioned really helped students achieve academic success—and emotional, self-esteem-building success as well. By reading to each other and to lower-grade students, they felt much better about themselves.

Cory, one of the reading students I taught in my early teaching years, called me a few years ago. He told me that I had made a difference in his life. I taught him that he could do it and achieve great things in life. He talked about going to college to become a teacher. His family was so proud of him. He is now teaching first grade in a school in southern Indiana. I once visited his class and it was one of the most rewarding moments of my life. Of course, I brought stickers, treats, and books for all the children to enjoy. We stay in touch. "Jill," another student I taught who was very shy and not sure of herself in reading, is now a kindergarten teacher. When I last saw her, she had her daughter with her, who also wants to be a teacher when she grows up. Educators just keep passing on the passion for teaching.

This I consider a giant breakthrough, leading and coaching a student from nonreading status to teaching first graders to read. Every once in a while, I touch base with my former student and ask him how he is doing. I have heard from the community that he is a well-respected teacher. It is always better to give than to receive.

Encouraging Literacy Is the Job of All Educators

Now that I'm a principal, I continue to encourage students and staff to grow in their learning. We have had several writing workshops with published authors helping teachers to grow in their instruction of writing best practices. Teachers have also developed an after-school monthly Book Club. I like to take opportunities to read to students as often as possible. Encouraging literacy is the job of all educators, especially those who are in leadership roles. I hope my story will inspire and help educators fire up struggling students. You never know how much impact you can have on others!

Ten-Year-Olds, Tapes, and the Epiphany

Sheila Gaquin

The next day when I handed out the recorders and blank tapes, the kids quickly dispersed around the room and began quietly talking into the machines. I felt like doing cartwheels.

I WENT TO THE ARCTIC TO TEACH, but I was so miserable that first semester I nearly left. My fifth graders were bored, angry, and disruptive; I had no idea how to reach them.

Desperate, and without any expectations, one day I asked my class, "What do you appreciate about being Eskimos and living in this village?" After a very long uncomfortable silence, one hand went up. Then several more. My students were responding, and I could hardly breathe as I listened to them describe their lives. After school that day I scrambled to find tape recorders. I so hoped my students would want to record their stories.

The next day when I handed out the recorders and blank tapes, the kids quickly dispersed around the room and began quietly talking into the machines. I felt like doing cartwheels. That evening when I listened to the tapes, there were a few rude noises, but for the most part, I heard simple, honest narratives— a window into my students' world. I typed all of them.

I learned a lot that day. I learned that kids who've struggled in school need to begin on familiar ground with a task they believe they can achieve—in this case telling a story rather than writing it.

I was pretty sure the kids would be pleased to see their words on paper, but I was unprepared for the depth of their response. After I handed out the papers, most of the kids sat quietly reading their stories to themselves, and reveling—as authors do—at seeing their words in print. Then they read their stories to each other . . . multiple times. For once I didn't want class to end. Finally, one boy asked me if I'd write an A on his paper. I shrugged and said sure, and then was startled when the whole class jumped up. They all wanted A's. I nearly cried. I'd never imagined that these tough kids cared about letter grades.

I learned a lot that day. I learned that kids who've struggled in school need to begin on familiar ground with a task they believe they can achieve—in this case *telling* a story rather than writing it. I learned that just about everyone wants to succeed, but reaching for success is risky business when you've experienced mostly failure. I learned that listening can be a far more powerful teaching tool than talking. And I learned that I love my work.

Crackled with Honesty

That afternoon the kids proudly took their A papers home to show their families. It had been a great day, and I'd like to tell you that it was smooth sailing after that, but of course it wasn't. There were still lots of tough days ahead, but over time the kids moved from tape recorders to paper. They wrote about everything—families, friends, tragedies, successes, dislikes, loves, hopes for the future—everything. Grammar, mechanics, and spelling were very rough to begin with, and slowly improved, though most never reached grade level. The content of their writing, however, crackled with honesty, and with wisdom that never failed to touch my heart.

Seven years later, that class gave me the greatest honor of my career. They asked me to be the keynote speaker at their graduation. I struggled for weeks to write a speech loaded with sage advice that expressed the pride and affection I felt for all of them. In the end I dug out a stack of their papers I'd been saving all those years. At graduation I simply read their pure and powerful words back to them. It was the very best I had to give them.

Why Art?

Monique Poldberg

*I had each student create a painting
depicting winter.*

ART AND LITERACY GO HAND IN HAND. Literacy can scaffold the understanding of art and art can expand and contextualize literacy. Literacy and art open our eyes to the world as well as to other places and times. The connection is natural, but the challenges are real. Curriculum demands, time constraints, and the variety of learners present in any classroom put limits on art, both production and appreciation. Nonetheless, my experience tells me that the well-placed use of art and its positives outweigh any possible negatives.

An art and writing project with the theme of winter, with specific visual arts and language arts goals, had a lasting effect on "Paula," a beginning language learner, and on "James," a student with Asperger syndrome. To level the playing field among my different learners, after discussion and sharing of visual images, I had each student create a painting depicting winter. During an oral sharing class session, Paula was able to verbalize the correct English words to describe her painting, while James was able to articulate a description of his portrayal of the northern lights. Both received clapping ovations from their peers and became success stories. This indeed, was differentiation without segregation, with team building included.

I also use art as the focal point of a lesson. Beginning with a big idea, I will narrow it further to a single topic (say, going from community to homes, plants to flowers). I find a personal connection for the students to use to make it their own (their home, a real flower). It's great fun to take a virtual field trip to an online museum (my favorite is the Smithsonian American Art Museum site, www.americanart.si.edu) to find fine and diverse art examples to show students.

I use a combination of creating class word lists with my students and having them keep individual dictionaries. We have a classroom atmosphere where everyone is looking for the best ways to describe their work.

Now my students create the art—construction paper collage, watercolor and crayon resist—I decide on media that I am comfortable with or have support in using. I strive to focus on learning "art vocabulary" as well as "content vocabulary." I use a combination of creating class word lists with my students and having them keep individual dictionaries. We have a classroom atmosphere where everyone is looking for the best ways to describe their work.

Once the art is created, I feel it is imperative that my students orally share their works of art—in pairs, in small groups, or with the entire class. I go back to the examples of Paula and James.

Then it's time to put pencil to paper! Students have come to my classroom asking, "Can we *finally* WRITE??!!" We have invested time in the pre-writing phases of art creation and oral rehearsal and my students know what they want to say! I choose the writing application most appropriate to the subject or the standards that I need to teach to my students. I use art as a pre-writing activity for poetry, and for descriptive, expository, or narrative writing. Sometimes I have students complete a compare-and-contrast sequence that starts by filling in a Venn diagram to compare their art with the "master's" and moving it to an expository paragraph form.

After each writing task, I allow for sharing, peer or teacher conference, and revision. I post or publish the art and writing together to give the children the audience they deserve. Their work has been in our classroom, the library, and the school office. In fact, James's art and writing (completed for a science unit) was selected to be shown at a local museum! His family told me that they would not have gone to the museum had it not been for his work being displayed, so not only did they celebrate his accomplishments, they also made a connection with our community resource as a result of his work.

What's the purpose? Can't I just accomplish this same thing by reading a story, looking at the pictures, and completing a worksheet? Will it have meaning and emotion? Just yesterday I was giving my seven-year-olds a practice multiple-choice test. The question required them to pick the correct punctuation for the writing of a list of items. A beginning language learner raised his hand and asked, "Isn't this like the time we wrote about our art project and listed the things we used?" Why art? Why not?

Teaching and Learning with the Arts

Art is not just motivational or an extra activity to do if I have time. I feel that it is important in enhancing academic achievement in other content areas. With thoughtful planning and practice, art can be seamlessly woven into curriculum to provide meaningful and lasting learning and teaching. Karen Gallas in *The Languages of Learning: How Children Talk, Write, Dance, Draw, and Sing Their Understanding of the World* (1994) provided me with firsthand examples of teaching and learning with the arts using her experiences as a classroom teacher and as a teacher-researcher. Gail Burnaford, with Sally Brown, James Doherty, and H. James McLaughlin, has provided the field with *Arts Integration Frameworks, Research & Practice: A Literature Review* (2007), a resource for those interested in learning about what has been written about arts integration, including a historical overview, definitions, research, methods, and practices. As I work daily with my young students and experience their genuine desire to create and use art, I am motivated to ask questions about what makes the arts work and learn more about including them in my daily teaching practice.

Reflections on the Breakthroughs

Susan E. Israel

THE JOY OF TEACHING IS REFLECTED IN the many unusual instructional activities described in these stories. What I found particularly interesting is the variety of sensory methods the teachers used in working with children who struggle in reading and writing, some of whom presented behavioral issues. In almost all cases the teachers drew from unconventional techniques to provide motivation. Very often it was not something that was planned—the technique was tried out of sheer desperation to help a child achieve and become more confident. The teachers did not go out and buy expensive teaching tools or manipulatives to help the children become motivated. Rather, they found practical and available resources and integrated them into their lessons.

It should be noted that while many of the teachers in these stories made use of informal pre-assessment observations, in some cases they engaged in formal diagnostic testing to identify reasons for their students' struggles. The students did not fit conventional diagnostic profiles. As Terry Atkinson pointed out in his story, the testing led to "more questions than answers." It is important for educators to understand that struggling readers may exhibit a variety of individual characteristics that cannot be plugged into the "learning disabled" label. In the stories, the students' reading and writing difficulties were often associated with behavior problems, lack of motivation, or lack of self-efficacy.

Breakthrough Elements

The teachers in this section share a common approach to instruction using a variety of multisensory methods. What this looks like in the classroom and during tutor sessions is completely different for each child. What is similar is the ability of the teacher to identify hands-on approaches that are of interest to the child and that provide motivation, not just to stay on task and pay attention but to actually make a difference in the way reading and writing gains are acquired.

Terry Atkinson, for example, used a variety of multisensory approaches but found Lego blocks, a set of tactile tools, to be the key in unlocking the literacy door for Benjamin, a boy diagnosed with learning disabilities. Benjamin was a child who desired to learn but was unable to make connections using traditional methods. By encouraging the child to construct elaborate structures and then describe them verbally, Atkinson was able to capture the details in writing. Benjamin dictated building details that grew in complexity from simple labels to phrases to sentences while Atkinson worked to show him the sound and symbol relationships. Finally, he succeeded in getting the boy to read about his own creations and eventually to write about them.

Nina Nilsson worked with Elizabeth, a gifted first grader who might have been misdiagnosed as learning disabled, by using sandpaper letters and visual memory strategies as scaffolds to learning. In working with children like Elizabeth, teachers need to understand the importance of using multisensory tools that are motivational and personal. Elizabeth is a child whose unusual visual and memory strategies enabled her to learn. What can you do to think differently about the types of visual memory cues you are currently using to teach children with intellectual disabilities?

In the story by Amelia Evans and Mariana Souto-Manning, the toddlers—frequently needing attention and feeling of closeness—became distracted by their own behavior. When the toddlers were able to use tactile as well as verbal and visual book stimulation, they become more engaged pre-readers. The reward, being close to the teacher, becomes a psychological motivating tool that increases attention and motivation with young children. Proximity of the teacher and the students is worth thinking about when dealing with children who become distracted by environmental stimuli such as book selection routines.

Marianne McTavish teaches us how to understand the importance of thinking creatively about how to use multisensory approaches to learning. What ideas can you learn from this story that will help you in your own teaching?

Mary Banta, for example, found success with her struggling fifth-grade boys by giving them tactile and visual tools based on their interest in racing, sports, and comics. Eventually, she was able to engage them in comprehension and writing tasks by having them read and then create their own comic strips.

Reading about the Eskimo children in Sheila Gaquin's story is exciting because we not only get to hear about the challenges teachers face in Alaska but how one teacher uses a variety of multisensory methods to motivate her students to engage in writing. Reflecting on this story, I am struck by the simplicity of the task and the enjoyment the students gained by recording their stories orally and then reading the transcribed versions to each other. It would benefit today's diverse classrooms if we thought more about the cultural values children bring to a learning task and what we can do to integrate cultural activities with multisensory strategies. Using tape recorders with today's techno-savvy children might seem boring, but if tape recorders are the only resource available to a teacher, they should be used to increase auditory learning. Of course, many new technologies are now available and I suspect that most children have access to devices such as cell phones that can easily become multisensory learning tools.

The young artists depicted in the final story by Monique Poldberg show that literacy learning can begin with visual experiences, moving to a variety of other sensory methods. Somewhat similar to Gaquin's use of tapes, Poldberg tapped into the visual and artistic sensibilities of her emergent readers by having them create pictures as a way to inspire them to engage in vocabulary building and writing activities.

An important factor that helped foster the breakthroughs described in these stories was the trusting relationship that the teachers established with the children. As the stories in Part Three show, it is important that we get to know our students before we can teach them. Once the bond of trust and respect is established, learning can take place and the teacher plays an ongoing and integral role in the child's development. Educators need to understand the importance of this bond and how long it takes to get established, because the current system sends students off to the next grade with a new teacher. The trust is lost, and it can be difficult for new teachers who try to intervene with the students using new strategies or teaching methods. Perhaps continuity in teaching students from grade to grade is something that should be considered.

REFLECTION QUESTIONS

- What creative multisensory approaches inspired you to learn when you were growing up?

- Why do you remember getting your first box of crayons when you were growing up?
- What type of interactive learning experiences do you offer children who struggle or need further motivation to learn?
- What does it look like to provide a variety of multisensory approaches to create interest and motivation while at the same time incorporating literacy learning?
- Think about one child you would like to help in reading or writing and find out what type of multisensory activities are motivating. What can you learn from the stories in this part to help this child?
- Have you considered taking a class in the arts so as to try new things yourself?
- Do you think motivation is essential in any person's ability to carry out a task?

Lessons Learned

A major conclusion that can be drawn from the stories in this part is the potential for multisensory experiences to benefit a variety of learners, including those at risk. It is important to understand that these experiences should emphasize more than one sensory pathway. Although individual students may initially benefit from a single-sensory activity that appeals to their particular learning style preferences at the time, teachers in Part Three ultimately incorporated and combined more than one sensory approach to engage and motivate students at cognitive and affective levels. Multiple and integrated sensory activities can be effective for supporting a particular literacy goal (writing a story, motivating an unmotivated reader, introducing sounds and symbols as a way to teach reading). They can also be of benefit when integrated into general strategies for teaching and learning. In fact, the primary lesson I gained from these stories is that we should provide all our students with more multisensory learning opportunities.

Ten Literacy Breakthrough Actions You Can Take Today

1. Invite parents and students to bring their favorite learning games and toys to school for a special treat.
2. Visit the local thrift stores in your area and collect Lego blocks. Have a parent wash them before bringing them into your classroom.
3. Collect a variety of multisensory items in your home that represent each letter of the alphabet and place them in resealable plastic bags. Use the alphabet bags when trying to reinforce sound symbol relationships during the early stages of helping children learn to read. Another item to collect and place in ABC baggies or envelopes would be brand name products. Research shows that children entering kindergarten know 300 different brand name products. Using brand names as an entry point to learning reinforces cultural and environmental sensory strategies to learning.
4. Have parents donate art supplies for an art station in your classroom.
5. Invite parents and grandparents to demonstrate their hobbies and allow students to learn something new.
6. In your classroom, label items used for multisensory instruction with words so that English language learners can learn vocabulary. Labels can go on art supplies, brushes, paints, crayons, fabric, clay . . .
7. Prepare a writing tools station and fill it with a variety of writing materials.

8. Evaluate your personal classroom library collection and check to see if you have a selection of interactive books that provide opportunities for students to touch, feel, or hear things related to the story.
9. Do you have a variety of leveled books?
10. Visit a local children's museum as a reward and enjoy all the hands-on exhibits with your children. Some museums have discounts on certain days of the week, so you might check before planning a trip to the museum.

Further Reading

When you're looking for ways to integrate appeals to a variety of senses into your lessons: *The Power of Pictures: Creating Pathways to Literacy through Art* by Beth Olshansky (San Francisco: Jossey-Bass, 2008), and *So Each May Learn: Integrating Learning Styles and Multiple Intelligences* by Harvey F. Silver, Richard W. Strong, and Matthew J. Perini (Alexandria, Va.: ASCD, 2000). In addition to published books, explore the many free and easy-to-access multisensory resources available online to support the literacy development of children, including those with special needs.

When resources are tight and you want to integrate technology and literacy-related materials: the International Children's Digital Library (http://en.childrenslibrary.org/) can be incorporated into your curriculum and used as a way to create multisensory activities that can go with the stories you select. This site provides more than three hundred children's books online, along with a search window for finding books on topics of interest. Some of the e-books have pop-out text features that allow you to enlarge the print and select the language.

When you want to celebrate children's written work: *Write Now! Publishing with Young Authors* by Karyn Wellhousen Tunks

Reflections on the Breakthroughs

and Rebecca McMahon Giles is a book I recently discovered that I think all primary teachers should have. This book provides a practical framework for supporting young writers (Pre-K–Grade 2) in authoring, publishing, and celebrating their work. The authors of this book believe that publishing student work is essential to encouraging and enabling young writers. In addition, if you are interested in locating wordless picture books, Weber County Library publishes a list of wordless picture books that will appeal to a wide audience—Pre-K through adolescence—see www .weberpl.lib.ut.us/content/booklists/sort/t/31. For older students, *Kid's Space* (www.kids-space.org/index.html) is a commercial-free Web site designed for students thirteen years old and younger. This site features many opportunities for students to publish collaboratively and independently for a wider audience on the Internet. The *Story Book* section showcases students' stories, poems, art projects, and other work. These online opportunities for publication will inspire teachers to create engaging writing lessons where students will see themselves as authors as they create and publish original work on the World Wide Web.

When you would like to start a book club with your peers who also teach in the primary grades and want to learn about multisensory instruction: A book that focuses on research-based strategies while at the same time providing meaningful and fun learning engagements is *Play and Literacy in Early Childhood: Research from Multiple Perspectives* by Kathleen A. Roskos and James F. Christie (New York: Erlbaum, 2008).

ENGAGEMENT

PART FOUR

Transformation

LEARNING TOGETHER

About the Stories

Susan E. Israel

THE FINAL PART IN THIS BOOK FEATURES STORIES where the teacher made a difference using a new strategy with the child's particular needs in mind. Approaches that are geared toward the learner and not necessarily to the teacher's task can be called "learner-centered" instruction. Through the stories in this part, you will see many of the ways learner-centered approaches can be motivating to students. When things do not work, it is easy for both teachers and students to become frustrated.

The teachers who share their stories in this part portray struggles in working with very difficult children, children who have had a limited number of school successes. The learning environments range from one-on-one resource rooms and small group instruction to full-size classrooms. Katie Sullivan's story focuses on a first grader whose parents would not allow him to repeat kindergarten despite the school's recommendation that he do so. Deborah Vessels describes working with a child struggling with auditory discrimination. Both Gina Goble and Gigi Brignoni talk about the challenges of working with English language learners. In other stories, the teachers talk about their difficulties in teaching urban students whose motivation to learn had been almost crushed by their lack of success in earlier attempts. Richard Oldrieve shows how he enabled a child to overcome oral language deficits while teaching the second grader how to read and write. Alexa Sandmann writes about a breakthrough with a student who was one of the "bottom 60" in his sophomore English class. Lori Berman Wolf writes about the transformation of a child who'd had the desire to read and write "squashed" out of him. As you will see, all the teachers who share stories in this section have learned to use new approaches as they try to promote learning.

Perseverance, Motivation, and Collaboration: The Tools Needed for Success

Katie Sullivan

I WOKE UP THE MORNING OF SEPTEMBER FIRST, 2006, in a panic: only five more days until the first day of school. I had recently completed my master's degree in literacy at Boston University and was getting ready for my first year of teaching. I had been hired as a first-grade teacher at the school where I had interned as a literacy specialist. The classroom was set up, anything that could have been labeled had a label, but now I was anxiously anticipating meeting my students.

Specialists and other teachers asked to see my class list. I quickly learned that a boy on my roster named "Justin" had been recommended for retention after kindergarten, but his parents had insisted on his promotion to first grade. Those who knew him told me that he would need a lot of literacy support. Although it would make some teachers nervous, I was excited about the challenge. This is what I had gone to school for; now I could actually put all I had learned into practice.

I met Justin at our "Meet and Greet Day" and saw excitement in his eyes. Justin had just completed a summer reading program,

141

and he was thrilled to be in first grade. Justin's parents immediately requested a meeting to get me up to speed on his background. His mother explained:

> When faced with kindergarten retention being advised by both Justin's very experienced kindergarten teacher and Mrs. Jewell [the literacy specialist with whom Justin had worked], we had to take a very hard look at our options. We researched and we made the very hard and scary decision to not retain him. We knew we were gambling and that our choice would imply really hard work from everyone (Justin, us, Mrs. Jewell, and Ms. Sullivan) and could or could not pay off. Thus, from kindergarten summer on we decided to invest in Justin to try to give him all we could.

Justin was the star of my summer program!
He was grouped with students at his level
and quickly soared to reading increasingly
difficult books.

It was that day, even before the official school year started, that our collaboration began. A few days later, Terry Jewell (a senior literacy specialist at Baker School), Justin's parents, and I all met to discuss how to best support Justin.

I administered the Developmental Reading Assessment (Beaver, 1997), in which Justin achieved a score of 1 (pre-primer level). Terry Jewell and I determined that he would work with her in a small group setting four times a week and in a guided reading group with me four times a week. Thus Justin would be receiving sixty minutes of explicit and focused small group literacy instruction four times a week.

I used a flexible group model (Paratore, 2000) for my literacy instruction. This means that students not only work in homogeneous guided reading groups but also have opportunities throughout the day to participate in community reading (everyone reading first-grade text), in literacy centers, and in independent reading time. With this model, students build on their literacy skills through participating in various centers, continue to build fluency through independent reading, have explicit instruction at their appropriate level, and have access to first-grade text. This model worked very well for Justin. He was very concerned about not reading at the same level as his peers. Being able to read grade-level text such as *Frog and Toad* with my support and partner reading was very exciting for him.

Justin was very motivated to learn to read and was still excited about the process. In January, Terry Jewell administered another reading assessment and we were a little surprised that Justin's score improved to an independent level of 4 and instructional level of 6. We met with his parents, who asked if they had made the right decision (declining retention) and inquired if he would ever catch up to his peers. I reassured them that we would continue to support Justin. His mom informed us that she would do even more work with him at home, and we kept in close contact. He continued to make slow and steady progress and by the end of the school year he was reading approximately eight months behind grade level (DRA level 12). We were happy with Justin's progress, but still felt that he could use more instruction and practice. Thus I recommended Justin for Brookline's summer school program, Project Discovery.

Justin was somewhat discouraged that he would have to attend summer school. I sat down with him and told him how

Perseverance, Motivation, and Collaboration

proud I was of him and reassured him that his hard work *was* paying off. He just had to be persistent. That talk and learning that I would be his summer school teacher set Justin at ease.

Justin was the star of my summer program! He was grouped with students at his level and quickly soared to reading increasingly difficult books. Justin, his parents, and I were so excited that reading was starting to click for him. Upon entry to second grade, his teacher administered the DRA and Justin achieved an independent level of 30 (beginning of third grade). We were all so excited (and a little disbelieving)! In the words of Justin's mom:

> Amazingly (as I am extremely aware that he could have tanked and been completely overwhelmed in first grade) and thanks to every single person in Justin's environment (as I try my best to help him but there is no way I could ever have done it without Ms. Sullivan and Mrs. Jewell's constant help and guidance), it paid off.

As I finish my second year of teaching, I'm glad that I had the opportunity to witness and help a struggling reader become an advanced reader. My message to parents, teachers, and students is *never give up* and *work together.* There was not one single person or program responsible for Justin's success. His own hard work and motivation, his parents' dedication to their child's academic success, and Terry Jewell's and my explicit instruction and collaboration persisting beyond the school year into a summer program helped him not only catch up to his peers but surpass them. This is something I kept in mind during my second year of teaching. I was much more patient with my students and with myself in allowing children time to develop. We often look for a quick fix, but determination, persistence, and motivation are the necessary tools for success.

Better Than a Base Hit

Deborah Vessels

I HAVE WORKED WITH MANY STUDENTS WHO STRUGGLE with reading, some dyslexic and some not. Of those I have tutored, "Jake" stands out. His remarkable improvement is just short of miraculous. Reading difficulties can look the same but originate from vastly different sources.

Initially, Jake came to me about the same time as another boy his age; entering first grade, their nearly identical reading readiness levels were worthy of great concern. Informal assessments indicated that Jake was dyslexic while his counterpart simply sported an insufficient knowledge of the phonetic code. Having been employed as a therapist in a dyslexia clinic, I had some tricks up my sleeve, but truthfully, I was as nervous as a cat in a room full of rocking chairs. Jake was as dyslexic as any child I had worked with, and I wasn't sure I could really help him. Beginning with a reliable phonemic awareness and phonics program, I added exercises for auditory discrimination, visual analysis, and visual aural digit span. A sight word list completed the game plan. Standing on the pitcher's mound, I blindly tossed every pitch I knew and prayed that after taking a swing at them all, Jake would find the one he could hit. I only dared to dream of a futuristic, ethereal home run.

My anxiety increased as I split the first Dolch list in half and experienced literally week after week in which Jake could not spell the word *at*. His self-esteem and mine were declining rapidly. Filling in the gaps at home, his mother plugged away, torturing the poor lad with those tedious visual aural digit span drills and geoboard activities. After many, many weeks, we were actually able to add the other half of the first Dolch list. In that time, Jake began to decode phonetic patterns and learned to "feel" sounds in his mouth. This augmented his auditory discrimination, allowing him to separate sounds for spelling and stick them back together for reading. Suddenly, the pace picked up. He began to read actual short storybooks that were carefully sequenced with phonetic patterns and sight words. We made it to Dolch list #2! Though he did his fair share of moaning and groaning, he's a tough little guy with a great sense of humor; he learned to laugh instead of cry and to forge ahead without giving up. It wasn't long until he was conquering sight word lists with twenty-five words in two or three weeks and was decoding words with digraphs, diphthongs, and final stable syllables.

My anxiety increased as I split the first Dolch list in half and experienced literally week after week in which Jake could not spell the word at. *His self-esteem and mine were declining rapidly.*

Expression to His Performance

Today, Jake is a second grader who can read almost anything I put in front of him that isn't ridiculously beyond his level; he charms me by adding expression to his performance. Remarkably, he gets through sight word lists more quickly than some fourth graders that I work with. Although spelling will never be his strongest subject, he does remarkably well; once in a while, a particular word will take him several weeks to conquer. Continually amazing his parents, teachers, and me, Jake is whipping through chapter books now and getting A's on spelling tests.

He's a true hero to all kids who experience reading difficulties and an encouragement to educators who think they are facing a hopeless situation. Here's to a doggedly determined player who finally hit one out of the ballpark.

"Cheeese!"

Gina A. Goble

I FEEL PRIVILEGED TO BE A TEACHER OF second-language learners. Every day brings something new and exciting to the classroom. Added to that, I get to work with eager first graders! There is never a dull moment. Some enter first grade reading or ready to read, but others have not yet mastered the alphabet or letter sounds. For anyone who thinks being a first-grade teacher is a piece of cake, it is not. But it is rewarding.

As the school year began, I quickly gauged the abilities of my children and realized that I had my work cut out for me. The children who were able to read were so far beyond their nonreading peers. One child in particular, "Liliana," was already frustrated with herself. Liliana discovered, almost immediately, that she could not read like some of the others. She also discovered that she did not know the letter sounds, and she wanted to read like her peers. I provided countless opportunities for her and others to "read" environmental print, sight words, and repetitive text, and praised them as they did so. But for Liliana, especially, this was not good enough.

As the school year got into full swing, Liliana tried harder than I had ever seen any child try. She practiced stories over and over again, wanting—desperately—to look at a word and actually know the sounds of its letters. I was quite impressed with her unwavering determination. Each day, despite her frustration, Liliana tried harder than the day before. And finally the day arrived!

We were sitting on the rug, doing shared reading, when she raised her hand and volunteered to read. Hesitantly, I called on her. I was cautious because she seemed to be very critical of herself, and I was just a nervous teacher, not wanting her to fail. Liliana began to read and though it took her several minutes, she made it through the short text. Upon finishing, she said, "I can read! Look, I can read too." She was grinning from ear to ear, as were her classmates. It seemed, at that moment, the circle of readers welcomed their newest member!

But reading still did not come easily, and more often than not, she felt disappointed with herself. I kept trying to tell her that she was doing well and these small steps she was taking would help her become a reader. But she had little faith in me and none in herself.

But reading still did not come easily, and more often than not, she felt disappointed with herself. I kept trying to tell her that she was doing well and these small steps she was taking would help her become a reader. But she had little faith in me, and absolutely none in herself. As I worked with her one-on-one, she accused me of helping her too much when I praised her efforts. It seemed that she spent a lot of energy focusing on my lack of criticism for her. I did not feel that criticism was necessary, as she was her own biggest critic. And even though I knew that as she mastered letter sounds and sight words, it would soon click together. But how do you explain that to a six-year-old who wants nothing more than to read? It was quite a challenge for both of us.

Besides trying to read when I was one-on-one with her, Liliana did not volunteer to read again. I encouraged her during shared reading, but she would just tell us that she could not read. One day she saw another child read for the first time and I could just see the frustration overwhelm her. I knew that she was wondering the same thing I was: how could this child, who did not even know the alphabet a short time earlier, read before she did. But what I observed was wonderful! It seemed like her frustration turned into an energy that I had never seen from her. And for the first time, I knew she was really going to make that connection and read.

A few days later, as we read a new story together, Liliana volunteered to read. I called on her and she read so perfectly that it brought tears to my eyes. She read, "Cheese!" (though she stretched that word for about three seconds and filled it with expression), "'I like cheese,' said the cat."

Everything Clicked

I think I was even more excited than she was. It was in that moment that I realized Liliana had been observing everything she could when it came to reading. She was making connections, and finally, everything clicked; fluently, full of confidence, Liliana read with more expression than I had ever seen! Seeing the ear-to-ear grin on her face, afterward, almost made every bit of frustration worthwhile.

As I work with a new group of first graders, plagued by television and video games, I think of Liliana and remind myself that there will be Lilianas in this group also. Liliana helped me discover that even though she seemed to be making no connections, it was quite the opposite. Liliana was a sponge, soaking up everything she could, and finally she emerged completely ready to read. From Liliana, I learned that it is never too late.

Working with first-grade children from backgrounds of limited or no English, I find it challenging to teach reading. I have used many tools as ways to help these students develop the foundation for reading success. For these learners, especially students like Liliana, I encourage strategies such as stretching the word (similar to the way she read "cheese"). We discuss how they can get their mouths ready to say the words, and we spend a lot of time on phonemic awareness activities. Comparing Liliana to other students I have taught, she was a challenge. But the way she flourished serves as a reminder that even strategies that might seem trite to us are foundational and necessary for our young readers.

Formulaic Writing Is Not for Everyone: Especially Gifted First Graders

Evangelina "Gigi" Brignoni

I forgot to trust my instincts and my
background experiences.

SINCE 1978 I HAVE TAUGHT IN BILINGUAL SETTINGS in two largely impacted school districts: Los Angeles Unified and Montebello Unified. My first three years as a novice schoolteacher I taught third grade—the students had received their literacy foundation and I helped them take off from there. Stories, essays, poetry, and writing newspaper articles were some of the genres the bilingual students experienced together. It was fun!

My fourth year I taught kindergarten and we painted, learned color words, practiced oral language in the house center, danced, and sang Spanish songs to develop rhythm, fluency, and enthusiasm for the heritage language. That was quite an energetic year! The students and I had developed an enthusiasm for Spanish children's literature via music, art, and dance; however, they were not reading the basic words or learning their alphabet by sight.

So I asked to loop with my class and I became their first-grade teacher. This was my learning year—this was the year that I learned how to teach first-grade Spanish readers how to read and write. In 1981 we had very few Spanish materials, so I invented where I could. The students learned their color words by painting pencil outlined drawings I had sketched on butcher paper. My bilingual first graders were still painting and the paintings were from the Spanish children's literature books I found, which were English books translated to Spanish. After they read their books, I applied the language experience approach. My students would dictate to me what they liked about the book. I would then scribe their ideas, and they would trace the words and then rewrite them. They did this for a few months and then suddenly or developmentally they started producing print on their own. Simple at first—but they did not have to wait for me anymore, and they all were writing. By the end of first grade they were readers and writers. I heard only great feedback from their second-grade teacher.

There was much more written on his paper, but he read his story just like the other first graders in the class. He did not want to appear different and I felt very sad and devastated!

Fast-forward twelve years: I am in a new school district where I had taught sixth grade for four years. For personal reasons, I sought reassignment at an elementary school and the only vacancy was a bilingual first grade. I took it willingly, especially since I had such great success with my previous first-grade class—I should do just as well.

In contrast to my first experience as a first-grade teacher, I found many Spanish print materials—every student had a Spanish reader and the school library had plenty of Spanish children's literature on its shelves. There was plenty of literacy support in the first language. However, because I had taught upper grades for so many years, I forgot to trust my instincts and my background experiences. I sought expert help on how to inspire my first graders on how to write and grow in their writing. So I called the bilingual resource teacher in the district office. She gave me sound advice on how to begin and what writing prompts to use. Per her suggestions, I created writing packets for the students by stapling first-grade writing paper in sets of ten sheets with a green construction paper cover. I showed them how to date the paper and gave them a writing sentence frame that was: *Me gusta* _____ (I like _____) and then they were expected to finish what they liked.

In that class, I had a gifted first grader who loved to write and wrote like a brilliant fourth grader. His stories had descriptors, precise language, and bounding energy. He wrote about the family visiting the zoo, traveling to Mexico, receiving presents and celebrating family birthdays with lots of details, for example. We celebrated "Author's Chair" and when he started reading everyone listened. He knew how to write before he entered my room. After he read, other students read their stories and every story sounded the same—*Me gusta la pizza; Me gusta la hamburguesa; Me gusta el color rojo;* and so on and on. I would comment and say, "*Muy bien, a mí, también, me gustan las hamburguesas.*" Very good, I like hamburgers, too.

My gifted first-grade student continued writing his elaborated stories; however, one day, when he went to the front of the room, he started to read just like the other first graders: he said, "*Me gusta el zoologico* (I like the zoo)." His draft did not state that. There was much more written on his paper, but he read his story just like the other first graders in the class. He did not want to appear different, and I felt very sad and devastated! That was the day I ended the *Me gusta* stories and went back to what worked in the past—the language experience approach. Fortunately, most of the students were writing fluently by the end of the school year, and my gifted student blossomed once more and wrote and wrote.

Facilitating the Writing Process

It is important to remember the growing pains that later turn into success stories. I narrate this painful recollection because it transformed my way of reaching younger students, which ultimately brought more joy to my facilitation of the writing process in the primary grades. This story is also a reminder that there are many different learners and we educators should never try a one-strategy-fits-all approach in any classroom. Sentence frames and formulaic writing can assist some students, but my literacy breakthrough confirms that it takes a plethora of strategies to motivate the young and developing writer.

TRANSFORMATION

Spelling, Reading, and Writing Give Joey an Unexpected Voice and His Teacher and Classmates Inspiration

Richard M. Oldrieve

FOR FOURTEEN YEARS, I taught students with learning disabilities in a Midwestern urban school district. One success story—the one that gave me the confidence to begin writing for journals and presenting at national conferences—began early on a September morning, when a second-grade teacher introduced me to a student who had just been transferred into her room. The teacher pointed out that "Joey" didn't seem to be able to talk very well, and that Joey would also be receiving services from the speech pathologist.

Experience has taught me that the best way to assess a newcomer's abilities is to fit the student into the classroom routine and observe what happens. Consequently, it wasn't long before I had Joey join a group of students doing a Small Leap Spelling lesson. As per Hatcher, Hulme, and Ellis's (1994) *phonological linkage hypothesis,* each Small Leap Spelling lesson has three sub-parts that take five to ten minutes to complete. One focuses on phonemic awareness, another on spelling, and the last on reading words.

First, each student is asked to name some words that rhyme with a target word. For those at square one, I always begin with *cat*. Second, students are asked to spell the words they have just named. The words are called out one by one, and students try to invent-spell the called-out word. For students who struggle with what Torgesen (1988) terms *phonological processing disorders*, I limit the list to words in the *cat* family that begin with consonants that can be held and elongated. For example: *sssssat, fffffffat, mmmmmat,* and *rrrrrat*. After each word is spelled, I'll call on a student who has correctly spelled the word on paper or on a dry erase board to spell the word aloud (some students are still struggling with letter names and need the practice), while I write the word on the blackboard. Students who have made mistakes are encouraged to correct their misspellings. Next, the same list of five words is repeated in a slightly different order until all the students correctly spell the words.

Well, it quickly became apparent that Joey was going to keep saying tat. *In fact, he would have said* tat *no matter what I asked for, because* tat *seemed to be the only utterance he could pronounce.*

During the third section of the lesson, all the students are asked to read the words both in chorus and as individuals. Outside the time frame of the Small Leap Spelling lesson, students can be encouraged to read trade books that include the word

TRANSFORMATION

family words, or to write their own silly sentences and stories, or both (Oldrieve, 1997a, 1997b).

Joey's success with this lesson plan format was an inspiration not only to me but to other members of his group and class. During the first week of trying to name, spell, and read words that rhymed with *cat*, Joey would give *tat* as his rhyming word. Being a teachable moment type of teacher, I would then say, "That's good, Joey, but *tat* isn't a real word. Please try to give another word that rhymes with *cat*."

Well, it quickly became apparent that Joey was going to keep saying *tat*. In fact, he would have said *tat* no matter what I asked for, because *tat* seemed to be the only utterance he could pronounce.

Now, Joey might have been the group member with the officially diagnosed speech disorder, but all of the other students were struggling with naming, spelling, and reading the *cat* family words. Consequently, no one seemed to mind that during the second week we merely added a couple more *cat* family words to our spelling and reading list. The subtle but important sign that other students and I did notice was that during this second week, Joey might have kept saying *tat* when prompted to give a word that rhymed with *cat*, but his eyes and enthusiasm showed that he believed each of his responses was different. And thus the other students joined in with me when I encouraged Joey to keep trying because he was getting closer—especially in how he spelled the words.

By the fifth week, when this group of "phonologically impaired" students could rhyme, spell, and read all nine words in the *cat* family, Joey could also rhyme, spell, *and read* all nine words. And almost on cue, the next time Joey's second-grade teacher brought him to my room she asked, "What did you do to Joey? He now speaks so much I can't get him to stop."

Reciprocal Nature of Reading

So what are the morals to the story? First, students care about each other and want to see each other succeed. Second, speech is reciprocally related to reading and spelling, and learning how to spell not only helps students learn how to read and be more phonemically aware, it can help them learn how to pronounce words and annunciate.

This reciprocal nature of reading, spelling, and pronunciation is most obvious to literate adults when we come across someone with an unfamiliar name. For example, if we are trying to read a nametag at a party, we'll focus on the nametag while asking the wearer how to pronounce the name. If we are talking to a person on the phone and can't quite make sense of how to pronounce the name, we may ask for the spelling. And if we're trying to spell a name, we may ask the person to list some rhyming words that are spelled similarly. For example: even though my last name of *Oldrieve* originates in Old English and follows the adage of "*i* before *e* except after *c*," even my friends will struggle to spell it until I point out that the second syllable is spelled (and pronounced) the same way as the rhyming words *believe, retrieve,* and *grieve.*

Admittedly, many students may not need the linkages between phonemic awareness, spelling, and reading to be made with a program as intensive as Small Leap Spelling, but those who do are helped immensely. In addition to my personal experience with developing the Small Leap Spelling method and seeing it succeed with the students in my own class, I have received dozens of e-mails from teachers throughout the world who have read my article and wanted more information. Furthermore, I have conducted several studies in which Small Leap Spelling has been shown to work best at helping those students who scored below the pre-test mean (Oldrieve, 2005; Oldrieve and Pasquerette, 2006).

Teachers as Agents of Change

I will end on a recommendation for teachers to think deeply about. Teachers are the agents of change in any classroom and they drive the complex culture established within the walls of any learning environment whether it be at home or in school. That being said, the culture of every classroom that I envision is a caring classroom where teachers demonstrate respect for their students and students likewise demonstrate respect for their classmates.

"You Know Those Marks . . . ?"

Alexa L. Sandmann

He knew I hadn't given up on him because
I warmly welcomed him back.

I WAS TEACHING TENTH-GRADE ENGLISH WHEN "Darin" began to think of himself as a writer and a reader. "You know those marks they put around words when people are talking?" he said. "That's what I need to know how to do for my story."

Resounding in my head and heart for nearly thirty years now, these were the words I had longed for. Darin had finally taken me up on my offer to be included in the "literacy club" (Smith, 1987). For my part, he was always in; for his part, he wasn't sure he wanted to belong.

Darin was one of twenty in a class of sophomore English students. I had three classes like his, the "4s" as they were called, the bottom sixty students. He and his classmates were challenges. Nearly all were biding their time until they could go to vocational school the next year. Regular high school was something to be endured.

I wanted their year with me to be more than survival. I wanted them to become readers and writers. We began the year with a short story unit—just like every other sophomore English class. As part of our biography unit, we read (most of) Mark Twain's *Tom Sawyer*, watched a video of his *Life on the Mississippi*, and talked about career options. We read *Tale of Two Cities* by Charles Dickens, just like all the college prep sections. Okay, we didn't read Dickens's version; we had a sort of "classic comic book" version, but I did read aloud excerpts from the original, like the opening lines, "It was the best of times, it was the worst of times. . . . " They found the symbolism fascinating, and the details of the French Revolution riveting. Three-quarters of my students were guys, so fighting against the status quo and the use of the guillotines were topics they reveled in.

He snuck back into school to give me his childhood copy of Maurice Sendak's Where the Wild Things Are, *his favorite book. Why? He wanted to apologize for being a "wild thing" in my class. Who but a reader apologizes with a book?*

New and different materials kept my students working all year—except Darin. In March, I finally said, "Enough. I've used every strategy I know, and your behavior is now compromising your fellow students' learning. I can't allow that. Please talk with the principal." He walked to the office. He was sent to study hall for a week and told that after a week, he could decide whether or not he wanted to come back to class. He rejoined us. It seemed he hadn't given up on us—or me. He knew I hadn't given up on him because I warmly welcomed him back.

While his behavior wasn't perfect upon his return, he was within acceptable parameters. I believed in him and his potential—especially as I watched him write his short story. When I had initially invited the class to write a short story, a piece of fiction like we had been reading all year, he seemed to sit up a little straighter in his chair. "Can we write it on anything we want?"

"Yes," I replied, "as long as it's appropriate for school."

"Figures," he said, but he went straight to work that day and the next and every day we drafted in class. He even made a pretty good revising partner for a classmate, and then we came to editing. I feared the project would fall apart.

Instead, he asked me, "You know those marks they put around words when people are talking? That's what I need to know how to do for my story."

"You mean quotation marks?"

"Yeah. That's it."

"No problem. Let me explain."

Using his story as our text, I showed him how to place quotation marks, including the necessary commas, to set off the extensive dialogue in his text. It took all of five minutes, a mini-lesson at its finest.

When he turned in his story, his use of quotation marks was virtually flawless. It wasn't because I was brilliant, but because he—finally—wanted to know. It was *his* story that needed quotation marks, not some exercise in some book. Ownership changed everything for Darin.

Atwell (1989) was right; in order to create writers, we need to allow them time, ownership, and response. Darin had all three with me—time to write, make choices about what he wanted to write, and lots of responses from me and his classmates about his writing. Darin was an author.

Who but a Reader Apologizes with a Book?

How do I know he became a reader, too? After he was expelled in late May for smoking a cigarette on school grounds, he snuck back into school to give me his childhood copy of Maurice Sendak's *Where the Wild Things Are,* his favorite book. Why? He wanted to apologize for being a "wild thing" in my class. Who but a reader apologizes with a book?

Providing class time to read and write, honoring students' ownership in what they read and write about, and responding individually to both reading and writing efforts in the classroom make all the difference; this learning environment creates readers and writers. *Where the Wild Things Are* by Maurice Sendak is a great springboard to discuss students' fears about learning or fears about school in general. Use the book to begin a journal-writing activity. Here are some writing prompts to use: What are your fears about learning and why? Do you think you do other things to avoid the act of reading or writing? Why would you fear reading or writing today?

Nudging One Reluctant Writer into Action

Lori Berman Wolf

None of these reasons were the case with "Steven." Steven's mother called me one afternoon looking for help for him. Steven was having some difficulty in school and she didn't want him to fall any further behind his fourth-grade class.

I HAVE HAD THE OPPORTUNITY TO WORK WITH several students in the capacity of private tutor. Some of the most rewarding—and at the same time most frustrating—work that I've done is helping children who have lost the desire to read or write for one reason or another. A child who initially has some difficulty learning to read may fall behind the rest of the class, become scared to continue, and fall further behind. Or possibly the child is new to the English language and only gets to speak English at school. Perhaps the child has never been read to and doesn't own any books.

None of these reasons were the case with "Steven." Steven's mother called me one afternoon looking for help for him. Steven was having some difficulty in school and she didn't want him to fall any further behind his fourth-grade class. Steven attended one of the most prestigious private schools in his city. I agreed to meet with him a few times, assess his reading, and then make recommendations for either tutoring or for his mother to help him herself, if she wanted. I ended up working with Steven once a week for two years, including summers. Because Steven needed additional help with his schoolwork, many issues of fear and shame were present for him. This lasted for over a year of our sessions but began to abate during the second year.

He could write, but his writing was confined to a few perfunctory sentences, just enough to answer a teacher's questions about a book or a particular chapter. Writing was not only "boring" (code word for difficult), it was something he resisted in any way he could.

After testing and reading with Steven for a few sessions, I felt that he was overrelying on phonetic cues, while ignoring semantic and syntactic cuing systems (Goodman, 1987). He rarely self-corrected his miscues, even when the meaning of the story completely broke down for him. He could pronounce or "name-call" texts of varying complexity. Actually, Steven was a very good learner, doing what he had been taught to do. Yet, when asked to retell a story, he had difficulty. It appeared to me that he was reading on grade level for an average fourth grader. However, because of the school that he was in, the population in the school, and the level of work assigned, this would leave him at a disadvantage for understanding his class work and homework.

Looking at some of the class assignments and homework, I began to understand how Steven's desire to read and write had been squashed out of him. Assigned readings for his class were far beyond most fourth graders' comprehension: Greek mythology, complete with tales of preserving a young nymph's chastity (try explaining *this* to a ten-year-old boy), and F. Scott Fitzgerald's famous 1925 novel *The Great Gatsby* to mention only a few. These are wonderful books, but not when you are a ten-year-old child mostly interested in the Yankees, tennis, and golf. I can't imagine that the other students were able to complete these readings without assistance either. Classroom and homework response to literature was limited to questions about the story. Every now and then Steven had a written test, in class, based on the book. Of these questions, the majority required recall of detailed facts in the text, with few interpretive questions that would require different kinds of thinking (Bloom, 1956; Pearson & Johnson, 1978).

Reading became a chore for Steven and his grades began to fall. Steven was used to getting A's and wasn't satisfied with low B's. His writing was suffering too; his writing assignments also were receiving lower grades. He could write to fulfill an assignment, but his writing was confined to a few perfunctory sentences— just enough to answer a teacher's questions about a book or a particular chapter. Writing was not only "boring" (code word for *difficult*), it was something he resisted in any way he could.

Each week on my visit to Steven's house, I dreaded the greeting I would get. Sometimes a disgruntled boy would slump his way to the table where we were to work and plop down, lifeless, into his chair. This was when he had decided to be polite to me. Other weeks he openly announced, "Oh no, I'm not working for the whole hour. Take my sister for half of the time." or "Do I have to be tutored today?" I was not a welcome sight in Steven's house. Even a self-assured teacher could have her confidence shaken with the welcome I got from Steven every week for a year.

Tutoring a child after a full day in school when it is time to relax and watch TV, do homework, or play with a friend is not always the easiest task. We began our once-a-week tutoring sessions focusing on metacognitive strategies. My first aim was to get Steven to know when he didn't understand what he was reading and to stop and go back. I chose stories that were closer to his independent and instructional reading levels instead of constantly confronting him with frustrating reading as was the case in his class. Cynthia Rylant's animal stories in *Every Living Thing* were perfect for our first weeks of working together. The reading level is about fourth grade, and yet the content has many layers of meaning. One could interpret them as animal stories or dig deeper into their metaphors and messages. They worked very well for a reluctant boy who had been experiencing a great deal of confusion and frustration in all his reading at school. There was no such thing as reading for pleasure for Steven at that point. Maybe a baseball story or a *Sports Illustrated for Kids* article, but reading and pleasure operated in two completely separate spheres in Steven's mind. The whole idea of writing for pleasure was considered more than ridiculous. Writing was something that had to be done to fulfill an assignment. Any writing that I asked Steven to do was met with even more resistance than reading. Groaning and leaning back in his seat, politely defiant, he pleaded with me not to ask him to write. If I asked him to write down whether he liked the story he pleaded, "Can't I just *tell* you?" If I asked him to write down the answers to questions, he would try to give them verbally. Or he would write one or two answers and then finish the rest verbally. Writing was difficult and to be avoided.

Diana Mitchell and Leila Christenbury (2000) talk about some of the techniques that teachers use to create a conducive writing environment for our students. Some of the principles of good teaching practice that they identify as essential are student engagement (including interests and background), explanations and modeling, collaboration, and meaningful work (pp. 7–9). I had included many of these principles during our sessions together, and yet Steven still was not interested in writing. I wrote him a letter each week, hoping to get him to write back to me when we had our session together. I decided that we should start with dialogue or buddy journals (Bromley, 1989). We wrote for five minutes at the beginning of each of our one-hour sessions. That was five long minutes. "What should I write about?" Steven asked. He probably had never been asked to just write without being graded before. I told him to just write about anything that he wanted to write about. I suggested some initial writing starters on the first day but not during subsequent sessions: sports, what he likes, what he hates, or that he doesn't want to write. I wrote in my journal at the same time he did. This went fairly well for a few months until I asked him if he liked writing in the journals. "Not really," he answered. "Well," I told him, "I really like reading about what you are doing, let's continue for a little longer." I went home, discouraged as I frequently felt after our sessions that first year. Where was the spark that I usually managed to ignite? How would I find it?

How many teachers are willing to admit to stooping to new lows to get their students to display a desired behavior? I believe this is more commonly referred to as rewarding good behavior or positive reinforcement (Skinner, 1974). M&Ms to increase the length of time a student sits? Stars on the reading chart? Pizza party for good behavior? Playtime in the park for a period of

Nudging One Reluctant Writer into Action

hard work? I have been guilty of all of these maneuvers at different points in my career.

One day I was shopping in a drugstore when I noticed that some new types of pens were on the market. Milky pens. Gel pens. But the most exciting part was black paper pads to write on with these exciting pens. They are found now in most drugstores and stationery stores. I went for the gimmick. Ten gel and milky pens and one notebook with black paper, one with purple paper and one with red paper later—I left with a plan. I certainly didn't expect this gimmick to be greeted enthusiastically, and yet it was. Steven chose the notebook with black paper and I chose the one with purple paper. (These are, of course, impossible to make copies of!) We shared the pens each week and after several weeks, Steven began acquiring his own collection of these pens. Steven enjoyed trying out writing with new instruments on a new color paper. I enjoyed it too. Steven approached our journal writing sessions with renewed interest and some spark that might be construed as enthusiasm. Over the next few months, we began to spend longer periods of time writing in our journals. Slowly the journals moved from buddy journals into story journals. We began using the journals for revising and writing drafts. Steven was now willing to put words into print, whereas before, writing truly was tedious and sometimes even painful. Initially he needed the support of using writing as an extension of a conversation between us. As he became more confident in his writing, Steven began to see his journal as a place to write stories and drafts for school assignments.

Research supports the use of a variety of writing materials to support emergent writers (Teale & Sulzby, 1986). The more varied a child's literacy experiences are, the stronger the interest in literacy learning seems to become (McCormick & Mason, 1986). In Steven's case, I was able to see the importance of using varied materials with this developing writer. The materials acted as one of his motivations for writing, simply to see the way the colors looked on the page. This worked until the act of writing itself became more motivating for Steven. Some of the literature on perception talks about the work of the eye, hand, and brain during the process of writing (Emig, 1978) but there is an absence of information about varying writing materials with older children in order to motivate them to write.

Two years after I had begun tutoring Steven, he told me that his sixth-grade teacher had assigned *Shiloh.* I happily trotted over to the bookstore, picked up a copy and read it immediately. Finally! A book for a child had been assigned. I thought of some fun response activities and made sure to have some writing planned. When I got to Steven's house and sat down, I took out my copy of *Shiloh* and he took out his. My jaw dropped. I should have known better. An adult book. Shelby Foote's *Shiloh: The Battle,* a studious and erudite description of events that occurred during the Civil War. Steven kept a positive working attitude and worked on understanding that book and even had brief moments of not hating it. I knew that Steven had made tremendous progress. He felt surer of himself and was confident about reading books assigned to him that were meant for adults. I was so happy for Steven that reading was no longer scary for him and hoped that one day he would feel that way about writing too. I breathed a sigh of relief when *Shiloh* was done. He made it through the book. We analyzed the format of his teacher's tests and prepared for them. I was pleased that I had figured out how to scaffold (Cazden, 1988, as cited in Strickland, Ganske, & Monroe, 2002). Steven's reading and writing instruction seemed to help him become a more independent reader and writer. He did well on the weekly tests he was given in school. One thing that happened that I thought was interesting was that Steven began to identify his own interests with what was being assigned in his classroom. His interest in American history was being developed. He started reading books on the Civil War on his own. He also became fascinated in biographies about past U.S. presidents. Writing was no longer scary. When assigned an essay or paper to write, Steven would use one of the organizational strategies or graphic organizers we had worked on, and frequently the paper was partially written before I came to help him. I sensed that, although he didn't love writing papers, he didn't dread it anymore. He was able to carry through the steps of completing the assignment on his own. He had become more comfortable with expository text and the structure of expository essays (Moss, 2004; Goldman & Rakestraw, 2000). Writing narrative stories was still a chore; Steven never developed a taste for story writing during our time working together. After the second year of working together, Steven and I said good-bye to our tutoring sessions. His mother tells me that he did very well in seventh and eighth grade. Am I suggesting a causal relationship between milky pens and Steven's writing development? No, but I am suggesting that sometimes the right material, whether it is a book, pen, or magazine—in combination with sound instructional techniques—may be the impetus a child needs to begin the journey into the literacy club (Smith, 1987).

Motivation is essential in any person's ability to carry out a task. Somehow the novelty of milky pens was able to lead Steven into writing, where he found he could perform the tasks that his teachers demanded.

Teachers as Learners

This anecdotal evidence suggests the need for controlled experimental studies examining the impact of novel writing materials on students' attitudes and writing productivity. Additionally, qualitative studies describing the transition from one journal format to other journal formats may help to uncover some of the questions about why teachers choose to change writing instruction and how that responds to the needs of their students.

Reflections on the Breakthroughs

Susan E. Israel

THE MESSAGE REVEALED IN THE STORIES IN THIS section reminds me of someone who really motivated me to learn more when I was young: my fourth-grade teacher. My friend and I decided we wanted to write a book instead of using our spelling words in sentences, so we asked our teacher for permission. Our wish was granted, and the result was a book titled *Happiness Is . . .* The teacher liked our book so much that she put it in our school library after having it laminated. She also had the librarian catalogue it so it could be checked out by other students. Our book was very popular and when I was in sixth grade the book was still in the library. That experience really motivated me to continue writing as I grew older. Now I write lots of books and I love it when they are made available for others to read. What teacher made a difference in your life and motivated you?

What I love about the breakthrough stories in this part is that they encourage working together to learn to read and write. The stories make me think about the many times I noticed a book that a stranger was reading and I became curious about it. In many cases, I would interrupt the reader to ask for more information about the book. Our conversation never ended before our time together did. I realized that people love to share and talk about books.

Breakthrough Elements

Katie Sullivan, a former first-grade teacher, incorporates community reading in the classroom with peers and on grade-level text,
as well as lots of partner reading. This intervention incorporates a
social aspect that Justin responds to in a productive way that increases his ability to learn to read. Deborah Vessels helps a first
grader whose self-esteem is declining because he's beginning to
think of himself as unable to learn to read. She helps Jake learn
how to "feel" sounds in his mouth. With repeated programs and
supports in the home, Jake demonstrates progress. Gina Goble,
who works with second-language learners in first grade, succeeds
in helping a six-year-old frustrated reader, realizing that encouragement and patience can be the best intervention strategy. Gigi
Brignoni, who has thirty years' experience in Los Angeles public
schools, teaches students how to read and write. One bilingual first
grader, who was considered gifted and could write at the fourth-
grade level, allowed peer pressure to limit his abilities. Brignoni
created writing packets based on advice, but all stories began to
sound the same. After she switched to language experience
approach, the gifted first grader returned to realizing his learning
potential. Brignoni states, "This story is also a reminder that there
are many different learners in each classroom and we educators
should never try a one-strategy-fits-all approach in any classroom."
Richard Oldrieve helps us understand the reciprocal nature of
reading, spelling, and pronunciation, while also showing us how
students can support each other in their learning. Alexa Sandmann
reminds us how giving students a sense of ownership in their
learning can set even underperformers such as Darin on the path
to both writing and reading. Lori Berman Wolf shows how novel
writing materials, in this case "milky pens" and colored paper, can
help open the door to literacy improvement.

What I found interesting in the stories in Part Four was the
ability of the teacher to help a child shift from a negative attitude

about a literacy task to a positive one. One comment made by Oldrieve is that as educators we need to understand that students care about each other and want to see each other succeed. This makes me think about why some students are a bit disruptive during learning tasks. Perhaps they want to remain cool and not look stupid because they know they are not so successful with what they are doing or learning. This is a new way of thinking about how to reach children, especially older students who seem to cause a lot of disruption during learning tasks.

Another point that is interesting to me is how teachers needed to work with other adults to help a child achieve their reading or writing goals. It was also important for the students to observe this taking place. Students need to feel that they are valued, and what happens with a more learner-centered approach to learning is that students automatically feel valued because the instruction becomes personalized.

What I would like to see happen in schools or in learning communities is more development of oral language skills at all ages. Oldrieve makes a good point about the reciprocal nature of literacy; oftentimes oral language is an overlooked but important key in unlocking reading and writing. If students can talk about something, can they read about it? If students can tell a story about something, can they also write about it?

REFLECTION QUESTIONS

- What do you do when things you try in your own life do not work the first time, or at all?
- What does it mean to you to be a positive and supportive role model when working with challenging students?
- How would a learner-centered approach change the way you teach today? Reflect on the questions in the overview to help you think differently about learner-centered instruction.

- Can you recall a moment when you were little and you and a friend learned something new together? How did this make you feel?
- What are different ways that you might help children interact with others to learn to read and write set? What do you think children might value about your list?
- What helps you when making decisions about changing practices?
- Do students offer advice about how they learn, or do they have opportunities to offer you advice?
- Do you think speech is reciprocally related to reading and writing?
- How can you embrace moments of student interest and find ways to be learner-centered?

Lessons Learned

The stories in this section used learner-centered approaches to motivate students. Increased levels of motivation became the foundation for students' ability to excel. One important observation is that the lessons learned by the teachers emphasize that successful learning conditions start with the teacher. The teacher becomes the agent of change.

Ten Literacy Breakthrough Actions You Can Take Today

1. Teach students strategies for working in small groups.
2. Make sure students know what the expectations are when working together and ask them to repeat these expectations.
3. Begin collecting wordless picture books for your classroom.

4. Make a list of the successes your students have achieved most recently. Share this list with your students.

5. Think about three prominent people you consider leaders. Use the Internet to locate information about their successes and achievements. Share the stories with your class during read-aloud time. Tell them that it is important to celebrate others' successes.

6. To help you understand your students, ask them to talk about why they like working in groups, or why not.

7. Tell a story to your students about an experience you had working with others.

8. Think about how you can help students who do not like to work with others.

9. Create teamwork strategies that you can integrate into daily classroom routines.

10. Divide your class into their favorite sports teams for a day and have a contest related to skills or strategies they are learning.

Further Reading

When you want a series book with characters that students who struggle in school can relate to: "The Fonz" (Henry Winkler) has written a series of books published by Scholastic about his life growing up as a child with reading and learning difficulties. These are real-life stories that will appeal to any child or adult who struggles in some capacity with learning. Instead of bringing in these books to show your students, tell them about the books and use this as a teaching moment on how to do research. They can learn about Henry Winkler and his acting success in the process. This will help them understand why he wrote the books for children who struggle like himself in school. You might even consider showing them a clip from one of his old episodes.

When you want a provocative book about how to motivate the young people you're working with: *The Dumbest Generation: How the Digital Age Stupefies Young Americans and Jeopardizes Our Future* by Mark Bauerlein (New York: Penguin Books, 2008) discusses ways to motivate students by changing the way we teach and think about learning. It explains the challenges teachers are facing and offers recommendations on how to continue to motivate students in the digital classroom.

When you need insight on working with students who speak different languages: *Learning to Read Across Languages: Cross-Linguistic Relationships in First and Second-Language Literacy Development,* edited by Keiko Koda and Annette Zehler (New York: Routledge, 2008) offers helpful suggestions on how to overcome the fears often inspired by a lack of knowledge relative to language learners. Among the instructional implications I found helpful are the discussions related to metalinguistic practices such as phonology and morphology across languages.

PART FIVE

Conclusion

Seven Pathways to Literacy Learning

Susan E. Israel

WHEN I ASKED THESE TEACHERS AND FORMER teachers for stories about accomplishing a reading success or a literacy breakthrough with students in their care, I thought I would receive stories about unusual intervention strategies or methods. What I received instead were stories about meaningful experiences the teachers wanted to share, times when they recalled helping an individual child overcome a particular learning hurdle. In almost all cases the students portrayed in the stories were struggling, at risk of falling behind, or coping with some type of learning difficulty that posed challenges for the teacher. The students were similar to those we see every day in classrooms across America regardless of the type of school: those with reading or writing disabilities, oral language deficits, or a fear of not being accepted by peers, and both English language learners and special needs students. Some students faced issues of transience and homelessness. Others were gifted but unmotivated. In almost all cases, the students had talents and abilities that had long gone unrecognized. The stories showed that regardless of the challenges, teachers can make it possible for their students to make progress and set themselves on the path to literacy achievement.

Although the teachers were eager to reveal how they were able to help an individual child or in some cases a group of students, it is important to note that the breakthrough they describe rarely happened in isolation. Collaboration was essential. Collaboration occurs when teacher and students learn from each other, when teachers learn from other teachers, or students learn from other students. The contributors were not out to gain acclaim for their instructional accomplishments when they worked with the students described here. The most important and meaningful gift they received was the breakthrough itself, the fact that the child was able to make progress and experience success in either reading or writing. I call this "A Reading Hero."

In portraying what students were like in real-world classrooms, the stories enable us to understand why the task of teaching literacy requires more than just instructional skills. It also requires more than amusing lesson plans filled with strategy applications. Teaching requires a certain mind-set and way of being that is derived from what a student needs to move toward success on a task coupled with knowledge related to achievement-generated goals. Think back to the two questions posed earlier in the book:

- What is the best way to teach reading to a struggling learner?
- What is the best way to teach writing to a struggling learner?

In light of the stories, developing answers might best begin by considering what is most important to the particular student. Certainly students want us to provide warm and inviting learning environments where they feel safe. The stories in Part One show why it's essential to get to know students well. Understanding individual students and how they learn is an important first step in teaching either reading or writing. The stories in Part Two show why it is important that classroom reading selections be personalized and geared toward the student's needs. By better understanding the learning style of your students, you can generate reading materials and resources that speak to that style. You also need to make sure that students have a say in what they are reading or writing about. The stories in Part Three show how hands-on, multisensory opportunities can enable children to become more involved in what they are learning. Activities that engage the child in visual, tactile, or other sensory experiences can provide an entry into the world of words and language. Above all, it is essential to understand that literacy breakthroughs start not in the mind but in the heart. The stories in Part Four show why it is important for teachers to awaken inspirational and motivational pathways to learning. Lessons geared to the learner's interests, along with collaborative experiences where students are encouraged to learn from each other, can lead to literacy success.

As the teachers in the stories discovered, any of the approaches described here can support students who struggle in reading or writing and also encourage them to take ownership for their learning. Is this how you would answer the two questions stated in the Introduction? Or would you interpret the stories differently and perhaps even ask a different question? Think about this as I begin to share with you how I have made sense of the stories and the literacy breakthroughs that took place. Based on the common themes and insights I have gained from all the stories, I offer here seven recommended pathways teachers can take to enable students to achieve literacy success:

Pathway #1: Be Open to Discovery

In reading the stories, I noticed over and over how passionate the teachers were about finding ways to connect with their students and how they seemed willing to explore any measure that would make a difference in a child's literacy learning. Although in some cases it seemed the teachers stumbled upon their breakthrough strategies almost by accident, they were often able to apply the strategies to other children in other circumstances. When I invited the contributors to submit stories, I did not ask them to write about effective practices they discovered accidentally. Recall, they were to share a success story where they felt progress or achievement in learning resulted because of something they did. However, many of the practices described in the stories were improvised or were discovered serendipitously.

Perhaps you recall a teaching experience of your own where something happened that was unplanned but seemed to work really well. It is important to ponder and share these types of experiences so you can learn from your accidental teaching discoveries—and others can learn as well.

Based on the insights reflected in the stories, I offer three suggestions that can help you become more open to teaching innovations:

- Do not be afraid to try something new with your students.
- Be open-minded about new practices, and when reading or listening to others, consider how their ideas might apply to your own situation.
- If something you try does not work, invite the children to tell you how it might have worked instead of just dismissing your ideas.

Pathway #2: Develop an "I Can" Attitude

What comes through clearly in all stories is that the teachers had an "I can" attitude. Often after various trials, the teachers came to realize they could make a difference in the student's learning either by changing their instructional approach or by changing their expectations about the student. Having a positive attitude about the student's potential helped them to be more active in pursuing alternative teaching practices, rather than limiting themselves to conventional instruction that was not working.

The stories also suggest the benefits of teaching students about having an "I can" attitude as well. You can show them what this means by modeling for them all the new things you can do. Scaffolding students in smaller task steps will help them gain a stronger belief that they can perform the overall task. Elements of "I can" attitudes appear over and over in the stories, where students are encouraged to perform tasks they are comfortable and familiar with. For example, in one story allowing a child to play with Lego blocks and validating his constructions helped him develop an interest in writing. Drawing from lessons offered in the stories, the following suggestions can help you get started in thinking positively about what you can accomplish with your students:

- When you begin to feel discouraged about a student or situation, make a poster that says. "I can." Place this poster in a place where you can look at it when you feel yourself thinking negatively.
- Make a list of all the great things you can do. Include your talents, interests, books you like to read, and things you like to do. Share this list with students who are feeling discouraged and ask them to generate a similar list.
- Avoid conversations that include "I can't" statements. That would include other teachers, parents, and students. Instill a sense of "I can" values in your daily routine and instructional goals.

Pathway #3: Cultivate Students' Trust

In many of the stories, one of the teacher's first steps in breaking through a learning barrier was to build a sense of trust with the student. Very often teachers used their personal experiences and interests to capture the student's attention. By learning what was important to the student and by sharing their own heartfelt experiences, the teachers were able to gain the student's trust. When I first started teaching at the university level, I jumped right into my syllabi and course expectations. I soon learned from some of my student evaluations with higher scores that students liked to hear about me, and they liked it when I told them stories about my teaching experiences. In sum, they liked to learn about things that were important to me because this helped them understand me more as a person and as their professor. In addition, it helped place some of my pedagogical values in perspective, which allowed them a window into my way of thinking. The teachers in the stories did something to try to allow the students to get to know them too, often by sharing a story or book of value.

Here are three suggestions to consider in helping you instill a sense of trust with your students:

- Make a list of the things that interest you that you think might also interest the students you are currently working with. Share artifacts related to your interests so students can really get to know you and what is important to you.
- Share with students special experiences that happened to you when you were their age. This will help them understand that you have had emotions or feelings that might be similar to theirs and will enable you to connect with your students in a more meaningful way.
- Don't be afraid to let students know when you think you have done something that did not work. Students trust you

more when you are honest with them and will be able to identify with you as a real person rather than as just a teacher who holds the keys to all the knowledge.

Pathway #4: Match Strategy to the Learner

When you feel valued or cared for, how do you respond? Do you think children value a caring learning environment that promotes learning geared toward their needs? In the stories in all four parts, the teachers didn't always teach reading strategies by using standard books and curriculum materials. Instead, the teachers first made an effort to understand the child's needs and then matched their instructional strategies to that student using a variety of methods, including personalized book selections, to achieve their goal. This might be considered a backward approach to teaching, but it is exactly what was done. Strategy matching was sometimes done intuitively because the teachers wanted and needed to help the students who were most at risk and in their care. Here are three things you can consider when working with struggling readers and writers:

- Conduct assessment as appropriate, but evaluate the findings in ways that take into account what the child needs to learn or achieve. Focus not just on the bigger and broader goals of reading and writing but the tiny steps necessary along the way to reach the bigger goals.
- Think critically and look at instructional problems or situations from varied perspectives. For example:
    I know I have a checklist of reading strategies that I need to teach to make sure the standards are met. In the past, I have started with teaching the first one on the list. I can

be accountable for teaching the standards at grade level based on how many I have checked off. I might also go about having a checklist for each child, listing the time and the strategies that I know need to be taught. This way I can match the strategy with the child's needs while at the same time tracking skills that I am expected to teach.

- Be flexible and pick up on teachable moments even if it means straying from your lesson plans momentarily. Match the strategy with the teachable moment. Keep in mind that one size does not fit all students, so when selecting or adopting materials, perhaps think differently before spending the money.

Pathway #5: Celebrate Achievements

Do you like celebrations? Do your students like celebrations? Almost everyone enjoys an opportunity to attend a party. As the teachers in the stories celebrated small successes, you can too. Students benefit when their accomplishments both small and large are recognized. Think about the many simple ways you can celebrate a literacy breakthrough with your student, class, and school community. Here are three of the things you can do to celebrate literacy breakthroughs:

- Keep a log of goals and achievements. After each achievement, invite students to select from a treasure chest stocked with books and other literacy-related things.
- Send a note card or e-card to your students and parents commending them for their progress.
- Invite your students to think of creative ways to celebrate accomplishments in your classroom, taking into consideration the time and resources guidelines you provide.

Pathway #6: Seek Wisdom from Others

In many of the stories, the teachers were often in contact with important people who supported the student in some way, usually parents or other teachers. It is valuable for teachers to seek out individuals who can offer wisdom and advice on how a particular student learns. It is possible to spend weeks at the beginning of a new school year or semester getting to know a new group of students well enough to develop strategies for each one. Don't be afraid to work with others to help you understand your students before the start of school.

Here are three ways you can include others in your instruction:

- Send a handwritten note to past teachers and invite them to share with you teaching strategies that worked for that particular child.
- Learn more about the child by working directly with the parents. In some cases this might also require you to teach them how to teach their child so that the student is not receiving contradictory instruction.
- Review the files and take notes of important names and dates in your students' past. Contact the people involved and seek suggestions. Remember that you do not have to do what they did. Your classroom is different, as is your instructional strategy, but learning from others can give you a head start when you want a literacy breakthrough to occur. In return, leave detailed notes to help the next teacher learn more about each child's strengths as well as needs.

Pathway #7: Make Teaching Personal

In many of the stories, gearing literature to the individual learner was a key factor for teachers in making personal connections with their students and that finally led to the literacy break-throughs. A big part of learning happens only when students are interested and attentive. By offering students appropriate book selections and integrated multisensory applications, the teachers enabled them to focus and achieve.

Very often it was unusual books such as wordless picture books or comic books that motivated the students to read or write. What we learn from the stories is that teaching is more than giving students a choice in reading materials or linking instruction with students' learning styles. It is about personalizing teaching for specific students, lessons, or skills. Personalized teaching requires instruction to be meaningful and valuable. Broader instructional goals are always kept in mind. Here are three ways you can personalize teaching today:

- When choosing literature selections, think about sharing something that is meaningful to you and tell students why. Ask them how they feel about the stories you want to share with them.
- Use observation as an assessment tool to gain more information about your students and how to personalize your instruction. What is it that students need today to learn today's skill or overcome today's learning barrier? Apply what you learn.
- Ask children to help you develop a personalized reader wish list.

Summary

All the stories in the book share common themes and ideas. From them, I have synthesized seven pathways that, in my view, can help teachers achieve literacy success with their students. My interpretations of the stories and recommended "pathway" practices might differ from yours, because we each bring our own level of knowledge and experiences, as well as our interpretations, to our reading. To me, the beauty of offering these stories and sharing the authors' insights and experiences is to create opportunities for teachers to learn from each other. Dialogue about what is working is very healthy and helpful for all. I welcome your interpretations of the stories and how you might apply the ideas to your own instructional situations. I invite you to share your stories with me. Please e-mail me at sueisrael@comcast.net or go to my blog at http://home.comcast.net/~sueisrael.

My hope is that the stories in this volume along with my own contributions will inspire you to think differently about teaching literacy and how children learn. Returning to the two questions posed in the Introduction, how do you think the contributors of the stories might answer the questions? If you kept a journal with written responses to the reflection questions at the end of each part, I encourage you to go back to what you wrote and think about how you might respond now. How would you now describe the best way to teach reading and writing to struggling learners?

In the Introduction you were also invited to use the stories to reflect on or write about literacy breakthroughs you might have experienced yourself. I would encourage you to return to those experiences and think about how you made a difference with an individual student or group of students. The authors in this book returned to early teaching moments, as well as more recent ones. How might you apply those breakthrough strategies to situations you are currently experiencing with students? The hope is that the lessons you have learned from the stories in this book as well as your own experiences will enable you to set your students on new pathways to literacy achievement. I encourage all readers to document their teaching success stories and to consider sharing them with others.

The stories in this book have helped me change the way I think and react to the teaching of reading and writing. The pathways to success may vary from student to student. The pathway begins by building trust and developing personalized lessons and goals and is extended through collaboration. Be proud of your personal literacy breakthroughs. I hope the stories in this book will help you in overcoming barriers so that the very special child you are trying to reach can succeed.

References

Atwell, N. (1989). *In the middle: Writing, reading, and learning with adolescents.* Portsmouth, NH: Heinemann.

Auerbach, E., & Wallerstein, N. (1987). *ESL for action: Problem-posing at work.* Reading, MA: Addison-Wesley.

Beaver, J. (1997). *Developmental Reading Assessment.* Lebanon, IN: Pearson Learning Group.

Bloom, B. S. (1956). *Bloom's taxonomy of educational objectives.* New York: Longman.

Bromley, K. D. (1989). Budding journals making the reading-writing connection. *The Reading Teacher, 43,* 122–129.

Burnaford, G., with Brown, S., Doherty, J., and McLaughlin, H. J. (2007). *Arts integration frameworks, research and practice: A literature review.* Washington, DC: Arts Education Partnership.

DeFord, D. E. (2004). *Dominie Reading and Writing Assessment Portfolio, Part 1, 4th Ed., Kindergarten Through Third Grade.* San Diego: Dominie Press.

Elbow, P. (1998). *Writing without teachers.* New York: Oxford University Press.

Emig, J. (1978). Hand, eye, brain: Some "basics" in the writing process. In C. R. Cooper & L. Odell (Eds.), *Research on composing: Points of departure.* Urbana, IL: National Council of Teachers of English.

Fox, M. (2001). *Reading magic: Why reading aloud to our children will change their lives forever.* New York: Harcourt.

Gallas, K. (1994). *The languages of learning: How children talk, write, dance, draw, and sing their understanding of the world.* New York: Teachers College Press.

Gambrell, L. B. (1996). Creating classroom cultures that foster reading motivation. *Reading Teacher, 50,* 14–25.

Goldman, S. R., & Rakestraw, J. A. (2000). Structural aspects of constructing meaning from text. In P. B. Kamil, P. D. Mosenthal, & R. B. Pearson (Eds.), *Handbook of reading research* (Vol. 3, pp. 311–336). Mahwah, NJ: Erlbaum.

Goodman, Y., Watson, D., & Burke, C. (1987). *Reading Miscue Inventory: Alternative procedures.* Katonah, NY: Richard C. Owen Publishers.

Guillopp, A. (2005). *One scary night.* New York: Milk and Cookies Press.

Hatcher, P. J., Hulme, C., & Ellis, A. W. (1994). Ameliorating early reading failure by integrating the teaching of reading and phonological skills: The phonological linkage hypothesis. *Child Development, 65,* 41–57.

Keene, E. O., & Zimmermann, S. (2007). *Mosaic of thought,* 2nd ed. Portsmouth, NH: Heinemann.

Kohl, H. (1995). *I won't learn from you: Thoughts on creative maladjustment.* New York: New Press.

Lehman, B. (2004). *The red book.* Boston: Houghton Mifflin.

Leland, C. H., Harste, J. C., & Helt, C. (2000). Multiple ways of knowing: Lessons from a blue guitar. In M. A. Gallego & S. Hollingsworth (Eds.), *What counts as literacy: Challenging the school standard* (pp. 106–117). New York: Teachers College Columbia University.

McCormick, C., & Mason, J. (1986). Intervention procedures for increasing preschool children's interest in and knowledge about reading. In E. Sulzby & W. H. Teale (Eds.), *Emergent literacy: Writing and reading.* New York: Ablex.

Mitchell, D., & Christenbury, L. (2000). *Both art and craft: Teaching ideas that spark learning.* Urbana, IL: National Council of Teachers of English.

Moss, B. (2004). Teaching expository text structures through information trade book retellings. *The Reading Teacher, 57*(8), 710–718.

Oldrieve, R. M. (1997a). Success with reading and spelling. *Teaching Exceptional Children, 29,* 57–61.

Oldrieve, R. M. (1997b). Success with reading and spelling: Students internalize words through structured lessons. Available online: www.teachingld.org/teaching_how-tos/reading/default.htm. Access date: January 30, 2009.

Oldrieve, R. M. (2005, November 4). Does Small Leap Spelling help at-risk kindergartners develop phonemic awareness and beginning reading skills? Session presented at College Reading Association conference in Savannah, Georgia.

Oldrieve, R. M., & Pasquerette, E. (2006, November 30). CVC spelling development in kindergarten students: Is the achievement gap caused by misalignment between research, assessment, and methods? Roundtable discussion at the National Reading Conference in Los Angeles, California.

Paley, V. G. (1997). *The girl with the brown crayon.* Cambridge, MA: Harvard University Press.

Paratore, J. R. (2000). Grouping for instruction in literacy: What we've learned about what works and what doesn't. *California Reader, 33,* 2–10.

Pearson, P. D., & Johnson, D. (1978). *Teaching reading comprehension.* New York: Holt, Rinehart & Winston.

Shor, I. (1992). *Empowering education: Critical teaching for social change.* Chicago: University of Chicago Press.

Skinner, B. F. (1974). *About behaviorism.* New York: Vintage Books.

Smith, F. (1987). *Joining the literacy club: Further essays into education.* Portsmouth, NH: Heinemann.

Stepanek, M. (2002). *Heartsongs.* New York: Hyperion.

Strickland, D., Ganske, K., & Monroe, J. K. (2002). *Supporting struggling readers and writers: Strategies for classroom intervention 3–6.* Portland, ME: Stenhouse.

Teale, W. H., & Sulzby, E. (1986). *Emergent literacy: Writing and reading.* New York: Ablex.

Torgesen, J. K. (1988). Studies of children with learning disabilities who perform poorly on memory span tasks. *Journal of Learning Disabilities, 21,* 605–612.

Index

ESL classrooms: challenges of, 152; diversity in, 149; further reading about, 182; learning breakthroughs in, 7–10, 150–152; perseverance in, 149–152

Evans, A. C., 98, 109–111, 131

Every Living Thing (Rylant), 170

Expectations, of students: with emotional disturbances, 12; importance of, 189; who are struggling, 89–90

Expecting, versus waiting, 7–10

Experimental writing, 74–75

Exploration, as part of learning structure, 70

F

Fears, of students, 166, 173, 174

Field trips, 126

Files, of students, 193

Fitzgerald, F. S., 169

Flexible group model, 143

Foote, S., 173

Ford, M., 4, 29–31

Former students, 119

Formulaic writing, 155, 156

Fox, M., 109

Frye, E., 45, 55–57, 88

G

Gallas, K, 128

Gambrell, L. B., 93, 101

Games, for learning, 13, 118

Ganske, K., 173

Gaquin, S., 98, 121–123, 131

Gifted students, 100, 155

Giles, R. M., 135–136

Girls, 94

Goals, of students, 91

Goble, G. A., 139, 149–152, 178

Goldman, S. R., 174

Goodman, Y., 168

Gordon, C., 93

Gowin, D. B., 113

Grade-level texts, 169, 170

Graphic novels, 85, 86

Graphic organizers, 22, 84, 127

The Great Gatsby (Fitzgerald), 169

Group instruction, 142–143

Grow, L. P., 45, 73–76, 89

Guided reading, 142–143

Guillopp, A., 64

H

Harste, J. C., 15

Hatcher, P. J., 157

Helt, C., 15

High school students, 163–166

High-achieving students, 73–76

Holm, D. T., 45, 81–86, 89

Homogeneous groups, 143

Honesty: of students, 123; of teachers, 190–191

Hulme, C., 157

Human rights, 12

Humility, 35

Humorous books, 49–50, 61, 88

I

Identity, of students, 31

Imagination, 57

Independent reading, 70, 111

Inquiry, 70–71

Instincts, of teachers, 155

Instruction: common concerns in, xiv; in early childhood literacy programs, 115–116; for emergent readers, 27; for students with brain injuries, 18–19; for students with dyslexia, 145; for students with emotional disturbances, 12–15. *See also* Teaching strategies

Instructional level, of text, 169, 170

Instructional materials: for bilingual students, 154, 155; further reading about, 135; to instill a joy of reading, 83, 85–86; for multisensory activities, 129; for writing, 172–173, 174

Intentionality, 114–115

Intergenerational literacy programs, 113–115

International Children's Digital Library, 135

Islam, 21–24

Israel, S. E., xviii, 3, 33, 43, 87, 97, 129, 139, 177, 185

J

Janes, L., 45, 77–79, 89

Jewell, T., 142, 144

Johnson, D., 169

Joke books, 50

Jorgensen, K., 45, 59–62, 88

Journals: for independent writing, 77–78; motivation to learn and, 14; for poetry writing, 76; reluctant writers and, 171, 172; writing prompts for, 166

Joys of reading: in bilingual students, 60–62; for boys, 77–79; further reading about, 93; individual choice and, 61;

motivation to read and, 49–50; using comics to instill, 83–86

K

Keene, E. O., 63

Kersey, S.E.D., 38–39

Kid's Space (Web site), 136

Kindergarten classrooms, 153

Kindergarten retention, 141–142

Kindle, K., 3, 4, 7–10

Knowledge, of students. *See* Students, knowing

Koda, K., 182

Kohl, H., 12

Kucan, L., 93

L

Language experience approach, 154, 156

The Languages of Learning: How Children Talk, Write, Dance, Draw, and Sing Their Understanding of the World (Gallas), 128

Learner-centered instruction, 139, 179

Learning: barriers to, 33; games for, 13; human right to, 12; seven pathways to, 185–194; of story authors, xii; structure for, 70–71; student-directed, 70–71, 73–76; students' interest in, 13–14, 22–24, 27; students' ownership of, 14, 15, 165; trusting relationships in, 22

Learning breakthroughs: celebrations of, 33; definition of, 1; elements of, 34–35; in ESL classrooms, 7–10, 150–152; of intentionality, 114–115;

for, 87; questions for reflection on, 90; student interest and, 78, 169, 170, 174. *See also* Reading

Motivation, to teach, 11, 12

Motivation, to write: of boys, 77–79; comics and, 83–86; publication as, 177; students' interests and, 73–76; wordless picture books to increase, 55–57; writing materials and, 172–173, 174

Multisensory activities: benefits of, 97; definition of, 97; to encourage literacy, 118–120, 121–123; further reading about, 135–136; guidelines for use of, 133–134; importance of, 187; questions for reflection on, 132–133; simplicity of, 131; strategies for, 134–135; for students with brain injury, 18; for students with learning disabilities, 105; teachers' role in, 130–131; that incorporate art, 125–128

Museums, 126

Muslim students, 21–24

Muth, J. J., 92–93

N

Name-calling texts, 168

Negative attitude, 189

Nilsson, N. L., 98, 103–107, 130–131

O

Observation, 194

Oldrieve, R. M., 140, 157–161, 160, 178

Olshansky, B., 135

One Scary Night (Guillopp), 64

Online resources, 126, 135, 136

Opinions, of students, 78, 79

Oral language skills, 179

Oral perspective, of learning, 97

Outdoor read-alouds, 110

Ownership, of learning, 14, 15, 165

P

Paley, V. G., 13

Paratore, J. R., 143

Parents: collaboration with, 142, 143, 193; formal assessments and, 68–69; in intergenerational literacy programs, 113–115; intuitions of, 103; listening to, 103; students' separation from, 26

Parsons, D., 44–45, 47–50, 88

Participation, in class: engaging literature and, 65–66; in ESL classrooms, 150; lack of, 47–48; in poetry writing, 75–76; in research projects, 84

Pasquerette, E., 160

Patience, 8

Peabody Picture Vocabulary Test, 68

Pearson, P. D., 169

Perception, 173

Perini, M. J., 135

Perseverance, 141–144; in ESL classrooms, 149–152; of students with dyslexia, 145–147

Personal narrative, xiii, 30

Personal reflections: about transformations of learners, 179–180; on book selection,

Reynolds, P., 38
Rhyming, 158, 159
Roehrig, A. D., 38–39
Roskos, K. A., 136
Rylant, C., 170

S

Safety, in the classroom, 13, 14, 57
Sandmann, A., 140, 163–166, 178
Scaffolding, 57, 189
School language, 61, 62
Science, 106
Scieska, J., 93–94
See the Ocean (Condra), 39
Self-esteem, 57, 119, 146
Sendak, M., 166
Sensory writing, 73–74
Sentence frames, 155, 156
Sentence starters, 50
Sequencing skills, 18, 118
Shared reading, 70, 151
Shared writing, 56, 65
Shiloh: The Battle (Foote), 173
Shor, I., 11, 13
Short stories, 165
Sight words, 105, 146
Signs, 114–115
Silver, H. F., 135
Silverstein, S., 55
Simplicity, 131
Skinner, B. F., 171
Small group instruction, 142–143
Small Leap Spelling lesson, 157–159, 160
Smith, F., 174
Smithsonian American Art Museum, 126
So Each May Learn: Integrating Learning Styles and Multiple

Intelligences (Silver, Strong, and Perini), 135
Souto-Manning, M., 98, 109–111, 131
Spanish language, 154, 155
Speech, 157, 159, 160
Spelling, 8–9, 146, 157–160
Standards, for learning, 191
Stepanek, M., 73, 89
Story starters, 50
Story webs, 22
Story writing, 165, 174
Storytelling, 122
Strategies. *See* Teaching strategies
Stretching words, 152
Strickland, D., 173
Strong, R. W., 135
Struggling students: activities to initiate creativity in, 118–119; with bad attitudes, 117–118; books about, 181–182; challenges of, 4; doubts about, 7–8, 9; with emotional disturbances, 12–15; engaging literature and, 65–66; expectations of, 89–90; in high school, 163–166; individualized instruction for, 100–102; learning breakthroughs of, 7–10; perseverance of, 141–144; reading levels for, 169, 170
Student-directed learning, 70–71, 73–76
Students: diversity of, xiii, 4, 185; fears of, 166; matching strategies to, 191–192; as teachers, 21–24, 34
Students, knowing: to achieve trust, 132; assessment strategies for, 194; definition of, 3; doubts about, 7–8, 9; with

Visual memory, 106
Vocabulary, 93, 118, 126
Volunteering to read, 150, 151

W

Waiting: for children's responses, 63, 66; versus expecting, 7–10
Wallerstein, N., 15
Warzon, K. B., 38–39
Watson, D., 168
Weber County Library, 136
Wells, G., 25
Where the Wild Things Are (Sendak), 166
Winkler, H., 181–182
Wolf, L. B., 140, 167–175, 178
Woodcock Johnson test, 68
Word choice, 85
Word families, 158–159
Word recognition skills, 18–19
Wordless picture books: to motivate students, 55–57; selection of, 88; source for, 136; writing for, 64–65

Wright, P. T., 45, 63–66, 88–89
Write Now! Publishing with Young Authors (Tunks and Giles), 135–136
Writer's workshop: components of, 165; for teachers, 119–120; trust in, 21–24
Writing: about art, 127–128; about cultural background, 121–122; belief that students will participate in, 29–30; in bilingual classrooms, 154, 155–156; improvements in, 123; materials for, 172–173, 174; for pleasure, 170; purposeful, 116; story authors' use of, xiv; with struggling high schoolers, 165; students' fear of, 174; for wordless picture books, 64–65

Z

Zapata, A., 4, 25–28
Zehler, A., 182
Zimmermann, S., 63